T0346314

Zane Grey's
Riders of the Purple Sage

ZANE GREY'S
RIDERS OF THE PURPLE SAGE
The Real Story Behind the Wild West's Greatest Tale

STEPHEN J. MAY

TWODOT®

Helena, Montana, and Guilford, Connecticut

A · TWODOT® · BOOK

An imprint and registered trademark of The Rowman & Littlefield Publishing Group, Inc.
4501 Forbes Blvd., Ste. 200
Lanham, MD 20706
www.rowman.com

Distributed by NATIONAL BOOK NETWORK

British Library Cataloguing in Publication Information available

Library of Congress Cataloging-in-Publication Data

Names: May, Stephen J. (Stephen James), 1946- author.
Title: Zane Grey's Riders of the purple sage : the real story behind the
    Wild West's greatest tale / Stephen J. May.
Description: Helena, Montana : TwoDot, [2021] | Includes bibliographical
    references and index. | Summary: "When Riders of the Purple Sage was
    published in 1912, it set in motion the entire Western genre in books,
    movies, and eventually country Western music"— Provided by publisher.
Identifiers: LCCN 2020040591 (print) | LCCN 2020040592 (ebook) | ISBN
    9781493049011 (cloth ; alk. paper) | ISBN 9781493049028 (electronic)
Subjects: LCSH: Grey, Zane, 1872-1939. Riders of the purple sage. | Grey,
    Zane, 1872-1939—Influence.
Classification: LCC PS3513.R6545 R5363 2008 (print) | LCC PS3513.R6545
    (ebook) | DDC 813/.52—dc23
LC record available at https://lccn.loc.gov/2020040591
LC ebook record available at https://lccn.loc.gov/2020040592

♾️™ The paper used in this publication meets the minimum requirements of American
National Standard for Information Sciences—Permanence of Paper for Printed Library
Materials, ANSI/NISO Z39.48-1992.

Contents

Zane Grey during the filming of the first version of *Riders of the Purple Sage*, 1918

INTRODUCTION

When I am dead, let it be said:
"His sins were scarlet,
But his books were read."
                    —HILLAIRE BELLOC

HE HATED CONTEMPORARY LIFE. HE LOATHED BIG CITIES WITH THEIR noise, pollution, crime, corruption—and temptations. He avoided liquor but he wrote about swarthy hombres gathered in saloons over shot glasses of whiskey. He couldn't draw a gun, but he could fire a rifle as well as his desert comrades. Like many aspiring novelists he wrote for ten years before breaking through with a major publisher.

Zane Grey, born Pearl Zane Grey, created the prototype for the Western novel that was to last far into the twentieth century. *Riders of the Purple Sage* was his second book to meet with wide popular appeal. His first novel for Harper and Brothers, *Heritage of the Desert* (1910), gave him a platform, but it was *Riders* (1912) that lifted him to the best-seller lists and later to international stardom.

Over time its significance became apparent; however, it wasn't until the present century that its impact became fully recognized. This is the story of the background, creation, and success of the West's most famous novel. My other two books on the author, *Romancing the West* and *Further Adventures of Zane Grey*, explore Grey's many lives as a writer, traveler, fisherman, and adventurer. In this new book I seek to examine the seeds that were sown into the creative mind and relate how this novel became so cherished in our popular culture. Grey wrote over fifty novels. Why does *Riders of the Purple Sage* remain fascinating for generations of readers? I intend to answer that question.

I am not alone in judging the impact of Grey's novel. Western Writers of America and the New York Public Library have named it one of the most influential novels of the twentieth century. Additionally, *Riders* became more widely known through five motion pictures (1918, 1924, 1931, 1941, and 1996). In 2017, it premiered as an opera in Phoenix.

Such success was not always apparent, however. In 1912, Harper and Brothers, Grey's publisher for life, temporarily shelved the book, claiming its anti-Mormon views were too inflammatory. Themes of "blood atonement" and "sealed wives" were prevalent in many sensationalized accounts of the Mormon settlements in Utah. Grey's novel, reasoned Harper's editors, would only spread the wildfire. Eventually, Harper relented and the book achieved a spectacular rise in popularity, both for its merits as a novel and for the Western genre in general.

* * *

Several years ago, I had the chance to sit down and talk about Zane Grey with his son Loren.

We met at a convention in Zanesville, Ohio, Grey's birthplace. I had corresponded with Loren for several years, but this was the first time I could pick his brain for a whole hour. In many ways, Loren was the opposite of Zane. Loren was a professor of psychology at Cal State Northridge and a Western novelist in his own right. It was one of those warm, languid days, when the leaves nod intermittently and the sun seems to invite conversation.

Of course, we talked about Zane Grey. I wondered what it was like for Loren growing up in the shadow of a celebrated father figure, a writer of Western tales, an explorer, a womanizer, a traveler, a renowned fisherman, a sailor of the seven seas. Was there any pressure growing up in the Grey family? I asked Loren.

His response was brief: "It was murder," he said. I could have asked him to elaborate a little more, but the conversation soon turned to other facets of Zane's life. Besides, he had told me what I needed to know. The intensity of Zane Grey's life had deeply affected everyone who knew him, particularly his family.

Grey was notoriously absent from his family for many years. When Loren Grey was ten years old and living in Southern California, Zane was skippering a ship heading to Tahiti and New Zealand. During this time, he wrote every day, sometimes from the cabin of his ship or up on deck under the shadow of a boom. He was in the South Pacific writing about Arizona, Utah, Wyoming, and Montana, about the Old West. Perhaps the wide, molten sea reminded him of the desert with its wastes and vast distances.

In many ways, the maturing of Zane Grey can be found in his early novels, most pointedly in *The Heritage of the Desert* and, of course, *Riders of the Purple Sage*. There is always something compelling about the artistic struggle. Perhaps we see ourselves in the writer's shoes, struggling to find just the right idea for a book or just the right characters and storyline that will guide us to success. Grey had the same struggles, although he had to compete with serious depression and troubling self-doubt.

But could he have written *Riders of the Purple Sage* without his demons? Probably not. Every writer and artist brings his weaknesses and strengths to bear on the work he is creating. Therefore, every work of art is imperfect in some way. It's just that some novels are better and more enduring than others; this is the case of *Riders of the Purple Sage*. It has proven to be a novel that captures not only the quintessential West, but also the West we want to remember. Most of all, Grey poured his entire self into the writing of the novel, which has made *Riders of the Purple Sage* timeless and fascinating over the years.

I think you will find that how the novel was conceived, written, edited, published, and adapted for five films is just as intriguing as Zane Grey's struggle to become a writer.

Finally, I would like to acknowledge the assistance of the Ohio Historical Society, Zane Grey's West Society, the New York Public Library, HarperCollins, the Zane Grey estate, the Cline Library at the University of Northern Arizona, and the Anschutz Collection of the American Museum of Western Art in Denver, the latter for permission to use the work of Frank Tenney Johnson. Johnson, along with Herbert Dunton, W. H. D. Koerner, N. C. Wyeth, and Douglas Duer, illustrated several Zane Grey titles during the 1920s and 1930s.

S. J. M.
Sedona, Arizona

Author's Notes:

Zane Grey's family name was spelled Gray. In his twenties he changed the spelling to Grey, which is how he is referred to throughout the text. Tsegi Canyon is located in northern Arizona. Zane Grey frequently spelled it Segi Canyon.

CHAPTER ONE

Grubstreet, USA

MANY ASPIRING WRITERS JUGGLE TWO VOCATIONS. THE MAIN OCCUPA-
tion is the one for which they were educated and the one that pays the
bills. The other vocation is held on the side and might luckily finance their
writing pads. The former keeps body and soul in some harmony, while the
latter feeds some deep creative urge. Most writers are able to keep these
vocations in precarious balance. And then there is Zane Grey, who rarely
balanced anything for very long. He wrote, he fished, and he loved. In
between he traveled. He readily gave up his first occupation to become a
writer in a world that was open to anyone with an idea and a typewriter.
Returning from his travels, he would head home to write the next book,
smelling faintly of desert mesquite or bluefin tuna.

But when he was twenty-four years of age, a writing career was far in
the future. In 1896 he graduated from the dentistry program at the University of Pennsylvania and set up a dental clinic at 100 West Seventy-
Fourth Street in New York, a short distance from Central Park. He had
received a first-class education at Penn, although he was the first to admit
he often did not pay attention in anatomy and biology classes. His mind
wandered frequently. While the professor lectured about organs and tis-
sues, Grey reflected on passages from Nathaniel Hawthorne, James Fenimore Cooper, and his favorite dime novelist, Charles F. Fosdick, known
by his pen name, Harry Castlemon. In English grammar classes, in which
he should have been studying intensely, he wrote stories about Indians
and settlers in his native Ohio. With intense cramming and some late
hours in the library, he was able to pass his final exams.

If he had pursued his dentistry occupation purposefully, Zane could have prospered in New York. Dentistry and oral surgery had made substantial gains with the advent of x-rays and general anesthesia. Local anesthesia, in the form of Novocain, was just on the horizon. Dentists were attaining the same stature as doctors and surgeons. With its burgeoning population, New York was a magnet for entrepreneurs, businessmen, lawyers, and doctors, offering its residents high salaries and attractive benefits. Alas, given his passion for writing, he could not force himself to dedicate his time to his primary career. He set up a desk in the rear of his clinic so that he could sneak away from the dentist's chair and write down his thoughts. At first he had no idea what to write about. He knew that authors were plentiful in New York and that they wrote for magazines and newspapers. In his first two years in the city, he tried to focus on stories that would sell. He had heard of demanding publishers who rejected beginning writers by the score, so he tried to write articles and stories targeted for certain periodicals.

He thought, naively at first, that writers were born talented and that publishers sought them out. Only later did he learn about the sacrifice, the hard work, and the tolerance of rejection it took for any person to succeed in the writing game. New York was filled with famous and wealthy authors, as well as a much larger number of hungry, unknown ones willing to endure the ups and downs of the writing game. This latter group populated Grubstreet, which was not a real thoroughfare but a state of mind.

The term "Grubstreet" originated in England in the eighteenth century; Samuel Johnson described it this way: "Originally the name of a street in Moorfields in London much inhabited by writers of small histories, dictionaries, and temporary poems; whence any mean production is called Grubstreet."[1] Since then it has symbolized any collection of writers who desire to sell their work for remuneration. It can include hack and pulp writers as well as beginning literary artists who turn quickly to cheap, commercial fiction to make ends meet. As the number of magazines, dime novels, and newspapers rapidly increased after the American Civil War, it particularly found a home in New York and the Atlantic Seaboard. The American author Upton Sinclair wrote that Grubstreet was "composed of thousands of newspaper men, magazine editors, and writers, poetry mongers, storytellers and novelists—for a large part people without the slightest knowledge of literature and without any idea whatever of literary tradition, but who have gone into writing as into any other trade, who study to know the 'market,' and who watch hungrily for any subject that will 'go'; who will turn you out a biography of a great man six weeks after he is dead, and who will watch the public taste in fiction and dash off a new romance or slum-study."[2]

The whole inscrutable world of New York publishing rattled and frustrated Grey for many years. His diploma hung conspicuously on his dental office wall, declaring that he had graduated from the University of Pennsylvania Dental Program and that he had been a student from 1892 to 1896. His education on Grubstreet, though not official, would last longer —much longer.

* * *

Like many beginning writers, Zane Grey desired a platform or something in his past to give him leverage with editors. He needed a feature to distinguish him from other writers. Jack London found it in the Klondike; Herman Melville acquired it in the South Pacific; Owen Wister discovered it in Wyoming and produced his seminal novel of the West, *The Virginian*, in 1902. Grey had not traveled to the Klondike, the South Pacific, or anywhere beyond the Ohio River. But he knew he had a famous heritage. Born in Zanesville, Ohio, in 1872, he claimed notable ancestors on his mother's side. During the Revolutionary War, Colonel Ebenezer Zane left Virginia with a ragtag militia and eventually commanded Fort Henry, on the site of present-day Wheeling, West Virginia. On one occasion, as British forces assaulted the fort, the colonel's young sister Betty Zane rushed gunpowder to the soldiers on the battlements. Dodging bullets and carrying the powder in an apron draped over her shoulder, she rushed from soldier to soldier, supplying them ammunition. The colonel later established Zanesville, among other towns. Grey often boasted that he was the proud descendant of the invincible Betty Zane. The Zane legacy in Ohio boosted Grey's self-worth throughout his life and gave him confidence in the worst of times.

Even during his mid-twenties in New York, he often turned to his boyhood dime novels for inspiration. Friends gave the adolescent Grey their used novels, which he slowly devoured in his bedroom. Much to the consternation of his demanding father, Dr. Lewis M. Gray, also a dentist, Zane kept a stack of them hidden in his closet under his flattened baseball mitt and fishing tackle. He used to stick one in his back pocket and sneak away to nearby Dillon's Falls to fish for chub and catfish. With his line dangling in the water, he passed the minutes reading passages from Harry Castlemon's *Frank in the Mountains*. In these pages were men and women of the real West. This is what adults surely did, he surmised. They left their desks and their offices. They rode out in the open air as free men and women. Clad in cowboy hats and chaps, they galloped over the countryside, roping cattle and cleaning up lawless towns. Their lives were far from the humdrum of Zanesville and were packed with derring-do, fistfights, brawls, and imperiled maidens. The heroes of that golden age answered to no one. He imagined it to be a glorious life and hoped maybe one day he could relate their stories just as his favorite authors had.

Soon Grey wrote his first story, "Jim of the Cave," a picaresque little tale that his father discovered and promptly tore up in front of him. Excoriated by his parent, he never forgot the black shame of that moment. He started writing in private, which prompted mixed feelings: in one moment he was jubilant and in the next he felt ashamed to be wasting his time.

The dime novels that nurtured Grey throughout his life and were the direct ancestors of *Riders of the Purple Sage* gradually lost influence as magazines and newspapers became more popular. In the 1860s and 1870s, however, Beadle and Company dime novel authors wrote of everything in the adventurous world: from jungle and borealis to the desert and open sea. A good dime writer could turn out a thrilling story of quick-paced prose of seventy to eighty typed pages in two weeks. Authors were paid between $75 and $150 for a typed manuscript.[3] Since a struggling writer could make a decent living from producing dime novels, publishers rarely lacked a ready supply of them. Crime, piracy, and historical fiction saturated the pages, but always leading the way was the Western. The deeds of Buffalo Bill Cody, Pawnee Bill, and Wild Bill Hickok populated the best-selling novels. As time went on, more female heroes, such as Calamity Jane, entered the genre. One Beadle writer, Prentiss Ingraham, after receiving the go-ahead from Beadle on a book proposal, remarked that he drew out his "trusty fountain pen, locked myself in, and working from breakfast to breakfast, completed my task."[4]

Beadle novelists usually kept the company's rules taped on their desk-tops. Among other demands were these: "(1) We prohibit all things offensive to good taste in expression and incident; (2) We prohibit subjects of characters that carry an immoral taint; (3) We prohibit what cannot be read with satisfaction by every right-minded person—young and old alike; (4) We require your best work; (5) We require unquestioned originality; (6) We require grace and precision of narrative, and correctness in composition; (7) Authors must be familiar with characters and places which they introduce and not attempt to write in fields of which they have no intimate knowledge."[5] Any writer who slipped on any of these requirements was rejected outright.

Despite these strict rules, authors flooded Beadle with stories. Perhaps the most famous of these writers was Ned Buntline, the pen name of Edward Zane Carroll Judson. He was a prodigious traveler in the American West and often boasted of his meeting with Buffalo Bill Cody, an encounter he wrote about in fourteen dime novels. In sum, Buntline pounded out nearly four hundred thrilling yarns of America and beyond. His writing process was unique in that he began with the title first. "When I hit on a good one," he noted, "I consider the story half finished. It is the thing of prime importance. After I begin I push ahead as fast as I can write, never blotting out anything I have once written and never making a correction or modification. . . . If a book does not suit me when I am finished, I simply throw it in the fire and watch it burn to nothing."[6]

The dimes and eventually the pulp magazines were the American heirs of Sir Walter Scott's Waverley Novels and shared many of the features of King Arthur's court. At the same time as Scott's novels were popular, James Fenimore Cooper brought the historical romance to America through his *Leatherstocking Tales* and his buckskin hero Natty Bumppo, or Deerslayer. The Western story, in particular, depicted the roamers and wranglers of the American West as knights of the range. A lawless land

Left to right: Adventure novelist Ned Buntline, hunter William F. Cody, and scout Texas Jack Omohundro

needed a code to live by, so the men and women adopted the chivalric system that was often demonstrated in the early and late Middle Ages. The knight—or Western hero—must not only demonstrate his bravery and fearlessness in battle but also uphold his beliefs in loyalty, fidelity, and honor. Self-knowledge, honor, and courage, even in the face of societal rejection, became the hallmarks of the frontier hero. Chivalry and courtly love were honored. Women were treated with respect, and frequently they appeared independent and savvy in their decisions. How men behaved in relation to women challenged Grey all his life, and it proved to be one of the most difficult hurdles in his fiction.

Breakthroughs in printing technology and demand for higher-quality material drove the creation of pulp magazines. In 1882 Frank Munsey started publishing *Golden Argosy*, a juvenile periodical, and later, in 1888, he created *Argosy*, one of the first magazines to spur growth in periodical readership. Other publishers followed quickly, abandoning the dime novel format in favor of a magazine measuring eight by ten inches and running 120 pages. The heyday of the pulps lasted well into the next century and included such titles as *Munsey's* and *Popular*, both of which Zane Grey tried to break into. *Popular's* tagline was "a magazine for men and women who like to read about men." At the same time, more prestigious magazines emerged, such as *McClure's*, the *Saturday Evening Post*, and *Ladies' Home Journal*. At the top end were the New York monthlies: *Scribner's*, *Harper's*, and *Century*, all of which remained beyond the reach of any fledgling writer on Grubstreet.

Assisting Zane Grey in his search for a publisher was the advent of the outdoor magazine. *Sports Afield* began production in Denver in 1887. *Field and Stream*, headquartered in New York, soon followed in 1895. *Outdoor Life*, also published in Denver, debuted in 1898. The trio became known as the Big Three and catered to a surging clientele interested in the natural American landscape. Because the offices of *Field and Stream* were near Grey's office, he frequently made contact with editorial staff, hoping for a bite. Nothing came of it until later, when he had established himself. In the meantime, he made the strategic decision to join the Campfire Club, an organization that promoted outdoor adventure and conservation. *Field and Stream* became the club's official publication, and it was through the latter that Grey met Eltinge Warner, who in 1906 became managing editor of the magazine.

* * *

On April 25, 1898, Zane picked up a copy of the *New York Journal* and headed toward his clinic. As he was walking, a headline suddenly grabbed him: "Congress Declares War!" He leaned against the nearest lamppost, scanning the front-page articles about the impending conflict with Spain over the sinking of the USS *Maine* in Havana harbor. At first he thought he might answer President McKinley's call for volunteers.

As always, he was dressed in a business suit, white shirt, and tie. He stood five foot, nine inches, and was well-proportioned and rawboned. Playing baseball on the side for most of his life had given him powerful upper body strength, a feature he would maintain later by landing marlin and tarpon in Mexico and tiger sharks in Australia. He had lank, dark hair and was clean-shaven. One remarkable characteristic was his intense stare, which seemed to bore right through you.

After thinking it over, he decided he was in no emotional shape for joining the military, but he decided to follow the journalists who covered the war in the *New York Journal* and *New York World*, the two competing newspapers that often sensationalized the conflict.

As the war escalated through the summer, one particular journalist rose to prominence and captured the attention of Zane Grey. Flamboyant and daring, Richard Harding Davis personified the new breed of journalists who were paid great sums to follow military actions and report them from the battlefield. William Randolph Hearst, publisher of the *New York Herald*, offered Davis $3,000 plus all expenses to cover the war in Cuba for the newspaper.

Dressed in his khaki uniform and tall boots, Davis accompanied the American forces into battle and wrote a series of dramatic reports for the paper. He was clean-shaven, a feature that in the late part of the century was somewhat prophetic. His image caused a cultural style change: beards, mustaches, and sideburns slowly disappeared. By the turn of the century, Davis influenced an entire generation of young males to rid themselves of facial hair.

Richard Harding Davis in 1900. Davis was the most famous and acclaimed journalist of his generation.

Davis's major contribution, however, continued to be his talent for reporting battlefield action in clear, gripping prose. Along with writer Stephen Crane, illustrator Frederic Remington, and a host of other journalists, Richard Davis covered the major skirmishes of the Spanish-American War in Cuba. He boosted the career of Colonel Theodore Roosevelt and in part made him a national hero. Writers on Grubstreet envied the intrepid Davis, seeing in him the stardom they wished for themselves.

* * *

For several years, Grey had experienced violent mood swings, resulting in deep depression followed by manic highs. Although he was never professionally diagnosed, he most likely suffered from bipolar disorder. At the turn of twentieth century, bipolar disorder, or manic depression, as it was known then, was little understood by the medical profession. All sorts of natural remedies were used to cope with the disorder, and people afflicted with it were viewed as lacking in morals because they often exhibited risky and dangerous behavior. Despite his condition, Zane persevered as a writer, even though the disorder often sent him into periods of dark, crippling depression. For days he was immobilized, unable to lift his pencil. He scribbled in his diary: "A Hyena lying in wait—that is my black spell! I conquered one mood only to fall prey to the next. And there have been days of hell. Hopeless, black, morbid, sickening exaggerated mental disorder. . . . It took a day—a whole endless horrible day of crouching in a chair, hating self and all, the sunshine, the sound of laughter, and then I wandered about like a lost soul, or a man who was conscious of imminent death."[7] He avoided alcohol, which in combination with his disorder would have proved deadly. He remained clean and sober for the rest of life, asserting that his strength and endurance came from a healthy body. His drinking friends often dropped by the wayside while he pressed on. During the darkest of dark hours, however, he struggled without help, without relief.

The one option that seemed to work was strenuous exercise, or hiking deep into the woods. In nature he found temporary solace. While in New York he would tear himself from the clutches of some black mood and head for the forests of New Jersey. He would run until he was breathless

Theodore Roosevelt in the uniform he wore for service in the Spanish-American War of 1898

and then retrace his steps, sometimes in the vain hope that his mood would brighten. He later would opt for more exhausting pursuits, such as wrestling fish, which he pursued from British Columbia to the Galapagos Islands. He loved fishing in the nearby streams. He and his brother R. C. had fished since boyhood, and often the latter would meet him halfway between Ohio and Manhattan. They frequently chose a spot on the Delaware River, Lackawaxen, Pennsylvania, which offered a pleasant and relaxing afternoon of fishing. Three years younger than Zane, R. C. proved to be a more durable baseball player than his brother; each boasted, however, their prowess as fishermen. For Zane, fishing was more than landing fish in a net. He liked to recline on the riverbank and let his mind wander. "I can stand a man to be a better angler than I am—which is hard to be," he deadpanned. "But as far as the dreamer end of it, I claim distinction."[8]

Avoiding the crowds in Central Park on weekends, he slipped across the bridge to play baseball for the Orange Athletic Club in New Jersey. During his stint in Orange, he switched from being a pitcher (his college position) to an outfielder, a change that another ballplayer named George Ruth happened to make several years later. Baseball was just another diversion that kept him from the routines and responsibilities of earning a living in his clinic. But the aroma of sweaty men and locker rooms was far better than the foul stench of infected gums and decaying teeth. Moreover, he simply did not like routines or responsibilities of any kind. "Reality is death to me," he once remarked. "I simply can't stand life as it is."[9]

In the years between 1896 and 1900, his writing rescued his sanity. Sometimes the words flowed easily onto the page. He kept a jar of sharpened pencils on his desk. When a tip broke or went dull, he put it aside and pressed on. He could go through four or five pencils for one article. When the words stopped coming, he rose and went for a walk around the block. Upon returning, he would stare at the blank pages of foolscap ready to be marked on. When necessary, he would attend a patient in the dentist chair. He repeated this process throughout his weekdays in New York. Up and down, back and forth. His mind frequently went blank; the pencil stiffened in his hand. He would simplify what he was trying to say, then resume his stint at the ironing board to press out the words that often wrinkled and resisted. His moments of extreme self-doubt produced a hesitant writer: "I am tortured before I begin to write, no call, no inspiration, no confidence, and no joy."[10]

He concentrated on writing sporting and outdoor articles, and on the side he penned several adventure stories in the vein of his favorite blood-and-thunder pulp writers. In 1902 he finally sold his first article to *Recreation* magazine, "A Day on the Delaware." In February 1903 *Field and Stream* published "Camping Out." Eltinge Warner, whom Grey had met through the Campfire Club, had recently become an editor at the sporting magazine and encouraged Grey to submit more articles for consideration. "My initial two articles boosted my self-confidence and supplied the inspiration to try other fields in writing," Grey wrote.[11] Frank Munsey, publisher of *Munsey's* magazine, told him to "keep the fishing stories coming, but also try your hand at fiction. It's a tough market to break into, but it pays well and the rewards are many. No westerns, though, unless you're Owen Wister or Hamlin Garland. They don't sell anymore."[12]

* * *

At the twentieth century's beginning many Grubstreet writers were reveling in the upsurge in magazine and periodical circulation. Markets previously depressed once again opened up. *Harper's Monthly, Harper's Weekly*, the *Saturday Evening Post, Collier's, McClure's*, and *Ladies' Home Journal* led the popular magazines. Additionally, the sporting and nature magazines, such as *Sports Afield, Field and Stream*, and *Outdoor Life*, enjoyed soaring circulation numbers. The pulps—*Popular, Recreation, Munsey's*, and *Outing*—benefited from the sudden interest in the natural world.

Many writers stayed on Grubstreet all their lives, turning out copy for such pulps as *Western Story, Detective Fiction, All-Story Weekly*, and *Ace-High*. Others like Frank Gruber and Alan LeMay moved on. Gruber left for Hollywood in 1943, wrote B movie scripts, and completed one of the first biographies of Zane Grey, in 1969. During his stint with the pulps, Gruber identified the nine basic storylines for the Western novel: railroad story, ranch story, small ranch story, vast ranch story, revenge story, cavalry and Indian story, outlaw story, marshal story, and dedicated lawman story. After he had worked out these classifications, "I could go over them," he remarked, "and decide that I had written stories in one or another of the groups only recently and it might be easier to do one of the others."[13] LeMay penned three notable books, *Painted Ponies*, *The Searchers*, and *The Unforgiven*, as well as several movie screenplays in the 1940s and 1950s.

A few Grubstreet authors left the street entirely when they were young and inevitably moved out of the entire neighborhood. At twenty-four years old, Jack London hit literary gold in 1900 with his collection of stories *Son of the Wolf*; three years later he hit it bigger with *The Call of the Wild*.

Zane Grey and Jack London seemed an unlikely duo to be swept up in a literary controversy, but that is exactly what happened. While Grey was targeting outdoor magazines for his articles, London, working three thousand miles to the west in California, was cashing in on his rambles in the Klondike and Alaska. Unlike Grey, London had no primary occupation to fall back on. His background included time as a vagrant, jail inmate, college dropout, gold prospector, and pulp master. He detailed his literary ascent with near blissful agony. He counted fifteen acceptances, while nearly ninety articles in every genre were rejected over four hundred times. For nearly two years, between 1898 and 1900, he studied the markets, read voraciously, sent out manuscripts by the dozen, and readied himself for the deluge of rejection letters that he kept pinned in a line reaching five feet high in his office. He imagined "a soulless machine" operating in editorial offices, sending out rejection slips. "A part of the soulless machine," he noted, "some cunning arrangement of cogs and cranks at the other end (it could not have been a living breathing man with blood in his veins) had transferred the manuscript to another envelope, taken the stamps from the inside and pasted them to the outside, and added the rejection slip."[14] Despite early failure, rejection, and often complete indifference on the part of editors, London pressed on, selling brief articles and stories here and there, most of which paid modestly. Luckily, though, he arrived at a time when colorful articles of lusty outdoor adventure were beginning to attract large readerships. After his *Son of the Wolf* soared in popularity, his sporting escapades in the north were eagerly sought out by *Harper's Weekly* and the *Saturday Evening Post*. London's literary territory included adventurous men and their animal companions trapped in a savage, primeval world.

Although London was widely praised for his nature stories, not all agreed with that assessment, including the naturalist and famed author John Burroughs, who called London and his followers "sham naturalists" and "romancers."[15] In a controversy that became known as the "nature fakers," Burroughs first chided Ernest Thompson Seton for asserting, in

Jack London (above) and Zane Grey traveled similar paths to literary success.

Wild Animals I Have Known (1898), that wild animals derive their abilities and instincts from humans. Writing in the *Atlantic Monthly*, Burroughs blamed Seton (and later London) for creating a "Yellow journalism of the Woods.... Fact and fiction are so deftly blended in the work that only a real woodsman can separate them."[16]

The controversy lasted for over ten years and pitted scientists and naturalists, such as Burroughs and John Muir, against the popular nature writers, such as Seton, London, and William J. Long. The former criticized the "romancers" of the woods for over-sentimentalizing animals in their natural habitats, while the latter fired back by claiming that their work was based on current scientific facts. London broke his silence on the matter in an article in *Collier's* magazine in January 1908: "I have been guilty of writing . . . two books about dogs. The writing of these two stories was in part a protest against the humanizing of animals, of which several animal writers had been profoundly guilty. Time and time again, and many times, in my narratives, I wrote of my dog heroes: 'He did not think these things, he merely did them.' And I did this repeatedly in order to hammer into the average human understanding that these dog heroes of mine were not directed by reasoning but by instinct, sensation and emotion, and by simple reasoning. Also I endeavored to create them in line with facts of evolution: I hewed them to the mark set by scientific research, and awoke, one day, bundled neck and crop into the camp of the nature fakers."[17]

As the argument raged and both sides fired salvos at each other, President Theodore Roosevelt injected himself into the controversy, siding with naturalists and scientists. Writing in *Everybody's* magazine in June 1907, Roosevelt saw no reason to romanticize animals since they were there to satisfy human needs. Called affectionately "a steam engine in pants" and caustically "that damned cowboy," Roosevelt was at first cautious about entering the debate, fearing that his status as president might make his participation seem inappropriate. But true to his nature, he criticized both William Long and London about inaccuracies in their writings. Roosevelt asserted that Long's books were "genuine crimes" against the nation's children. The president feared that Long's and London's books gave children an erroneous picture of natural history and called such writings "an outrage."

While Grey remained silent on the subject, Long, a respected clergyman, author, and naturalist, took aim at Roosevelt by calling him "cowardly" and a "game killer." Long's insults went further by claiming that "anytime he gets near the heart of a wild thing he inevitably puts a bullet through it." Thus, back and forth, the controversy dragged on through the first decade of the twentieth century. If nothing else, the debate raised awareness of humanity's relationship to the natural world and, in particular, to animals.[18]

It wasn't until 1908 that Zane Grey felt the impact of the debate, when he tried unsuccessfully to sell his short book *Roping Lions in the Grand Canyon* to Harper and Brothers. By then, the controversy had percolated down to magazine and book publishers. Harper's junior editors, fearing a backlash from conservationists, rejected Grey's manuscript, citing its mistreatment of animals. Eventually Eltinge Warner, managing editor at *Field and Stream*, accepted Grey's book and serialized it, beginning with the January 1909 issue. But by then it was clear that the "nature fakers" debate had shaped American sensibilities for years to come.

CHAPTER TWO

Beloved Infidel

THE PROPER INDIAN SPELLING WAS LACKAWAXEN, BUT LOCALS AND PIL-
grim anglers often called it "Lack-a-fishin," "Lack-a-rotten," or sometimes "Lack-a-women." But by any name, Pearl Zane Grey loved it for
its singular position on the Delaware River, just across from Delaware
House, a rustic hangout on weekends for jaded New Yorkers.

The diminutive Lackawaxen River flows out of the Pennsylvania Appa-
lachians and joins the Delaware River near the village of Lackawaxen. Grey
said of the river: "Winding among the blue hills of Pennsylvania, there is
a swift amber stream the Indians named Lackawaxen. The literal transla-
tion nobody seems to know, but it must mean in mystical and imaginative
Delaware, the brown water that turns and whispers and tumbles."[1]

In late August 1900, Zane's life of practicing dentistry, playing baseball, and writing underwent a seismic shift. Staying at the Delaware
House that summer with some friends was nineteen-year-old Lina Elise
Roth, who lived in Manhattan with her parents and was studying to be a
teacher at Hunter College. Grey met her when he and his brother R. C.
were rowing near the Delaware River shore. Within a few weeks Zane
and Lina became close friends and by the end of the year they were insep-
arable. Zane shared with Lina, called Dolly, his deepest desire to become
a writer, and perhaps he was attracted to her because she possessed all the
grammar and writing skills that he did not.

When Zane met and fell in love with Dolly, he set in motion the
features of romance he would represent in *Riders of the Purple Sage* some
twelve years later. Dolly helped lift Grey from a shy, withdrawn dreamer
to a man somewhat in touch with reality.

Midtown Manhattan in 1900 near Fifth and Park Avenues

EVERETT HISTORICAL @SHUTTERSTOCK.COM

For one thing, Dolly was a romantic too, but she had a strong maternal and practical side as well. She loved the classics of literature, especially Balzac, and she had a keen knowledge of grammar, syntax, diction, and tone in writing. That Zane was a dedicated, aspiring writer appealed deeply to her inner longing for art and expression. She followed his development as a writer and encouraged him to try longer works of fiction, perhaps even a novel. In her own right, however, Dolly represented the image of the modern woman, which instilled both love and fear in the budding writer.

In the first months of their relationship, Zane felt swept away by Dolly: "I never dreamed that I could love anyone as well as I have you. To be in your presence was delight to me." But in the same letter, he expressed how that infatuation had changed: "This is the simple entire truth. You have just told me that I was tired of you. So much for your understanding me. When we parted at Lackawaxen, my heart was heavy and I had a foreboding of evil as I feared those were the last of our happy days. We might have known that it could not last."[2]

By trying to be a breadwinner, a writer, a man, and a lover, Grey encountered some of the most turbulent days of his young life. He frequently rejected Dolly, the one person he loved the most, and in the next breath he wanted to be close to her. He was up one minute and prostrate the next. He often felt he was in a canoe heading to Niagara. Some gentle and supportive words from Dolly often set him straight: "A nature like yours," she wrote, "is one which fluctuates from the heights to the depths, and I know that to you the depths are very deep and dark . . . you yourself are not perfect. And have certain faults which may seem as heinous to certain persons as their characteristics seem to you . . . don't be discouraged. I am sure that I am not wrong when I say you will do something great someday. But make your aim the highest, if you fall short of that the first or second time, your effort will at least help you attain your goal." It was signed, "Your Dolly."[3]

Once in every generation, it seems, one man or woman arrives to shape the cultural identity of the era. Such a man was Charles Dana Gibson, who by the year 1900 established himself as the premier illustrator for American magazines and a beacon of hope for young women throughout the country and eventually the world. His most famous image—the Gibson Girl, as she became known—was a highly attractive woman with hair upswept and curls dangling on her temples. Her lips were firm and sensual, but she radiated an infectious self-confidence. She was dressed in long, flowing white dresses. Her image appeared on the covers of *Harper's Bazaar* and *Cosmopolitan* and attracted young women from age fifteen to forty.

Unlike the portrayal of the Victorian woman, someone generally subservient and homebound, the Gibson Girl was coltish, independent, and sexy without being sleazy, headstrong, vocal, and educated. As part of this revolution in gender roles, Dolly Roth enjoyed her young womanhood and being equal to any man she happened to meet. She possessed great self-awareness and a talent for languages. She encouraged women's right to vote, which was already on the books in Wyoming, Utah, Colorado, and Idaho. As the daughter of affluent parents, she could pursue her vocational goals without discarding women's traditional roles of homemaker and mother. As their courtship progressed, Dolly reminded Zane that he needed the balance that she provided. "Have I ever steered you wrong?" she asked. "It's my job to keep your feet on the ground while your head is in the clouds."[4]

* * *

By the early months of 1902, Zane was ready to begin a novel. He considered many options before selecting the story of his forebears, the Zanes in the Ohio River Valley during the Revolutionary War. Dolly told him to start it before the sweet bird of inspiration took wing and left him. And so, while still practicing dentistry in New York, he began *Betty Zane*. Dolly urged him on. Sometimes they met in the library of Hunter College, where Dolly got to see the novel as it progressed. Dolly relished this aspect of her relationship with Zane because it afforded her a level of intimacy that he denied her in daily life. On paper, she could see Grey's mind at work, his exuberances, idiosyncrasies, and moments of despair. She went through his manuscript, correcting faulty grammar and syntax and identifying unnecessary shifts in tone. Grey read her textbooks on style and began identifying his faults. "Think what the sentence is to exist

Dolly, seen here holding a prize bass, became Zane's wife, confidante, editor, and harshest critic.
COURTESY OF THE OHIO HISTORY CONNECTION P49_B05F02_001

for," he reminded himself, "what is it to exist for . . . do not change subjects if it can be helped. Cut out intensive expression and superlatives that are unnecessary . . . work for clearness, sequence, climax. . . . Brevity helps action and makes strength and force."[5]

Zane's mood swings, indeed his plunges, affected Dolly during their courtship. Her patience and self-confidence exposed many of Grey's vulnerabilities. His black moods caused endless problems in their relationship. When he was angry, which was fairly often, he lashed out at her over trivial interruptions. They would quarrel and not speak to each other for days. Later, his demeanor would warm into an impish smile and he would try to make things right. Often he would feel inadequate as a writer and hence as a young man trying to demonstrate that he could do something with his life. Revealing these insecurities to a young lady eleven years his junior was painful and threatening.

Throughout the autumn of 1902 and the spring of 1903, Grey worked ceaselessly on his first novel, *Betty Zane*. He wrote it in longhand, letting Dolly edit it for diction and consistency. She then turned Zane's scribblings into a suitable longhand copy. It was a fairly lengthy manuscript, nearly 100,000 words, and as time went on he would continue to write novels between 60,000 and 130,000 words.

During this period of writing fiction, he often threw down his pencil and turned to Dolly for support: "I think I have realized more than ever before what an utter impossibility it is for me to become a writer. What I have written would not have interested you were it not that you were interested in the man who wrote it." Dolly had previously admitted to Zane that she was not interested in American history, and therefore *Betty Zane* was of little importance to her. This crushed Zane: "That is the best criticism you ever made me; and it just about killed me. . . . You have time and time again, unconsciously put aside my opinions with contempt. It is not that you are right, for I feel this too, it is simply that I am a poor sentimental fool." In a moment of sheer despair, Zane wrote: "I do not want to be a great writer anymore. I wanted to write what I saw was the truth; truth about women and men. Not what I thought but what I know. And you have taught me that what I think and know could never be accepted by the world. . . . I wish to God you had never encouraged me at all."[6]

He managed enough confidence to finish his first novel, although he harbored deep cynicism about its commercial success. Before inserting the manuscript into a brown mailer, he wrote his name and address on a piece of paper to accompany his submission:

P. Zane Grey
100 West 74th St., New York, New York

On a mild spring day late in April he hand-carried his novel down Broadway and cut over to Pearl Street near the Brooklyn Bridge. He recognized the imperious headquarters of Harper and Brothers, Publishers, with its bold sign above the top floor. There was some method in his present madness. He knew that Harper and Brothers was the one of the premier publishers in New York, famous for authors who included Henry James, Thomas Hardy, Herman Melville, and Mark Twain. He succumbed to the delusion that he could be in such august company. He was convinced that no serious editor would reject his work. He strode through the doors and handed his manuscript to a nearby clerk. Grey stared briefly around the first floor with its warren of offices and the scurrying junior editors pacing in and out of them.

About a month later when his manuscript came back containing a brief standard rejection slip, he careened into despair. Dazed and stupefied, he began to believe that his writing was no good, and by some irrational extension, neither was he.

* * *

A Grubstreet hopeful, or any aspiring novelist in 1903 trying to sell his book, usually had to rely on his own legwork. Literary agents had not appeared in New York until 1893, when Paul Revere Reynolds opened what is believed to be the first agency. Reynolds sought the best writers of the time, including Jack London and Stephen Crane, hoping to use their fame to seek top dollar for their work. In 1907 Harold Ober opened an agency and added a few prominent authors. Due to the fact they were relatively new to the literary scene, agents usually hunted for authors, rather than vice versa.

Grey had no motivation to seek an agent. For one thing he didn't trust them. After a few weeks of bitter gloom over Harper's decision, he decided to hit the streets again. He delivered his manuscript to three publishers who in turn agreed to consider it. After rejections from Macmillan, Appleton, and Lippincott came in the mail, he fell into another period of despair and self-loathing. It was too much for Dolly, who also felt gloomy. Most novice writers were not aware that New York publishers made a business of rejecting good novels as well as best sellers, and based their decisions on the idea that it was the first fire of enthusiasm that sold a book. If an editor didn't feel the flame in his belly, chances are the book would not make it off the first floor.

Unwilling to see her fiancé sink any further, Dolly decided to dip into her inheritance money and pay for a reputable printer to publish the book. Zane agreed to help market *Betty Zane* himself. He resolved to do the legwork around Manhattan by delivering the book to reviewers and bookstores. His editor friend Eltinge Warner of *Field and Stream* suggested the Charles Francis Press, located on Thirteenth Street in Greenwich Village. Francis's company printed *Field and Stream* as well as other major magazines. Francis was reputed to be the best printer in New York and had built his business over the years by taking over the helm of failing printing houses.

As Zane and Dolly waited impatiently for the copy editing, printing, and binding to occur, Grey finished off his next book, *The Spirit of the Border*, the sequel to *Betty Zane* and the second of a proposed trilogy of books about the Ohio frontier. After his novel was again rejected by Harper, he took his failure more in stride. His confidence in himself had blossomed after penning two novels and he felt more comfortable in the narrative style. Creating character, setting, and plotlines came more easily, although he was the first to admit that fiction brought its own set of demands and frustrations. He felt less intimidated by the blank page—what Hemingway called the "white bull"—and in between keeping his dental patients reasonably happy, he could return to his writing task with more vigor and determination.

A. L. Burt and Company, largely a reprint house, agreed to publish *The Spirit of the Border* and his third novel, *The Last Trail.* It was not a big sale, but Grey was happy with it. Grey's spirit began to soar. He felt some surging current was taking him somewhere—to where, he did not know. But the mere presence of something positive in his life lifted him above his often crippling defeatism. He quit his job as a dentist. Zane and Dolly made plans to marry in late 1905, leave New York, and settle in a house in Lackawaxen, the place that they had first met. They would live on the rest of Dolly's inheritance and loans from Zane's brother R. C. until the day Zane's writing could start earning consistent royalties. Zane was glad to say goodbye to New York as a home base, to the crowds along Broadway and Fifth Avenue, and to the looming towers that stared down at him and crushed his spirit. Farewell to all that.

At some level, Zane felt that his writing career and his relationship with Dolly were slowly evolving into a permanent venture. As he looked forward to their marriage, he jotted down his feelings: "I have not the slightest fear. . . . What I shall be for you will make up all that I may have lost. You shall let me teach you all I know, and teach me all you know . . . You shall help me write literature, not thoughtless, careless books, but throbbing, red-blooded histories of life."[7] Dolly, the sensible, pragmatic one, revealed her wildest passions: "This morning I tried to get away from my love for you, to have a look at it. It seemed strange to me in that mood, that I should think of and want all the time, just one man in this great universe of people, that my happiness, my future, my life should be entirely dependent on him, on him alone."[8]

A month before their wedding, Zane felt it necessary to confess to Dolly that he still possessed a wandering spirit. In many ways, it foreshadowed much of his behavior in the following years: "I shall never lose the spirit of my interest in women. I shall always want to see them, study them, interest them. I never grow tired of women. Even my development has added tenfold to this fateful thing. Every woman raises my antagonism, excites my instinct of wonder and fear, and pity. Where I once wanted to break a girl's heart, with that horrible cruelty of the young and ignorant, now I want to help, cheer, uplift, develop, broaden, show things, and at the bottom still a little of that old fateful vanity. . . . I fear your strength. You are tearing my heart out by the roots, cutting, sculpting, remodeling my character at the expense of blood and flesh and old fixed institutions of hard set bones."[9]

This rather bold declaration on Zane's part should have alerted Dolly that she was dealing with a man who might indeed test her fidelity and possibly break her heart.

As their wedding day neared, Zane dashed off a note to Dolly: "Oh, Peaches and Crème! I don't really care about breathing the breath of life unless you are somewhere near. . . . I can't eat without you. . . . I can't do anything unless you are around. This is a vile, stale, profitless world without my doodle-dumkins. . . . I can't write such stuff as you write. It positively gives me a pain. . . . My need of you is greater than your need of me, in spite of all your protestations. You fill up a great void in my mind: all that longing and vain reaching out for God-knows-what is the better for you. This is a rotten pen. I have the darndest time with pens."[10]

On November 21, 1905, they were married and immediately burrowed into their house in Lackawaxen. Grey wrote a few outdoor articles and the two prepared for their honeymoon. In early January Zane bought two tickets on the Santa Fe Railroad heading to California via Chicago, Albuquerque, Flagstaff, and the Grand Canyon.

Nearing the age of thirty-five, he suddenly felt old. Without a paying vocation to fall back on, he had to prove to himself that he could be a successful writer and hopefully start a family. He also had to prove it to his new bride. But as their honeymoon trip neared, he had a moment of panic and uneasiness. "Tonight I leave for California with my wife," he jotted in his diary. "I don't really want to go. I don't seem to have the right feeling. I'd rather stay home. What will be the result of this trip? Shall I come back with a wider knowledge, a deeper insight, a greater breadth, or shall I simply be the same? I say—no! But then I have said no to many things. There is something wrong with me, with my mind, with my soul. Perhaps I shall solve the problem this time."[11]

CHAPTER THREE

Way Out There

TRAVELERS HEADING TO ARIZONA AND SOUTHERN CALIFORNIA IN early 1906 had one of two choices. They could brave the trip in a new automobile, such as a Cadillac Touring or a Ford Model C, but the way west was tortuous, muddy, and rutted from snow and rain. Before the interstate system was inaugurated and routes like 66 were completed and paved, the journey called for intrepid souls only. On the other hand, travelers could burrow into an Atchison, Topeka, and Santa Fe Railroad car and enjoy the scenery in style and comfort.

For their travel overland, Dolly selected the California Limited, a special Santa Fe train complete with dining car, lounge, and Pullman sleeper. After losing time in an unscheduled stop in Indiana, they arrived in Chicago with barely five minutes to catch the outbound train. Once settled in, they lounged and were astonished by the flat, frost-covered farmlands stretching to the horizon. Their first trip west produced mixed feelings of dread and wonder.

However, travelers who were not on one of the special trains out of Chicago had to endure numerous sojourns and delays along the way. By the time that Dolly and Zane took their honeymoon trip in January, the Santa Fe railroad featured several stops between Kansas and Arizona for the traveler to disembark and hit cafes, watering holes, and restaurants employing Harvey Girls.

Before dining cars were standard on American railroads, the Santa Fe and Fred Harvey created the idea that clean eating facilities on the route could boost tourism to the West Coast. Harvey created the Harvey House restaurants, acknowledged as the first restaurant chain in America.

Harvey aimed to replace the railside roadhouses that offered a plate of beans and dime-size portions of chipped beef or ham. In the late 1870s his so-called "eating houses" evolved into hotels, so that by the dawn of the twentieth century, he could claim a restaurant every hundred miles and a hotel nearby along the Santa Fe route. Harvey's attempt to create a diverse menu for the traveling public helped double the passenger traffic between 1885 and 1910.

In 1883 Harvey advertised in newspapers throughout the United States, looking for "white, single young women 18 to 30 years of age, of good character, attractive and intelligent." He promised room and board in addition to a wage of $18.50 a month. After they were employed, all Harvey Girls wore an immaculate black and white uniform: a dress that measured no more than eight inches from the floor, dark stockings, and black shoes. A house mother supervised them as they waited on tables and kept the traffic moving throughout the restaurants. They entered into a one-year employment contract that was usually only broken by marriage. The Harvey Girls were such a hit with the public that passengers anticipated each stop along the route.

Adding to the superb facilities along the Santa Fe route was the chief architect Charles Whittlesey, who assumed the role in 1900 at the age of thirty-three. Along with architect Mary Colter, he fashioned some of the most posh and utilitarian structures in New Mexico and Arizona. In Albuquerque, he designed the famous Alvarado Hotel, where Zane often stayed on his future trips out west. Located only a hundred feet from the train tracks, the Alvarado offered a Harvey House diner as well as comfortable overnight accommodations. In addition, Whittlesey designed the magnificent El Tovar Hotel, which opened in 1905 on the South Rim of the Grand Canyon. In mid-January 1906, the honeymooners arrived at El Tovar and stayed on the third floor, overlooking a hairline portion of the Grand Canyon. In her diary entry of January 15, Dolly noted the sun pouring light on the canyon rim: "It is a second inferno, stupendous, awe-inspiring, glowing with fiery colors."

Like Dolly, Zane was overwhelmed by color and sensation. As a writer growing in his perception of nature and its mysteries, he saw the world through more mature eyes. In January in northern Arizona, the

El Tovar Hotel, overlooking the Grand Canyon, still features the third-floor Zane Grey Suite.

sun, low in the sky, produces a light different from that in summer. The sun's rays heighten the reds and buff colors of the rocks, throwing much of the vermillion canyon walls into purple and blue shadows. He began to develop a language for this part of the Southwest, a language unique to time and place, and like no other in the world.

It snowed one day. The sagging sky was the color of slate. The drab, wet canyon, the skein of stone walls, and the layers of rock were suffused with blue, not a blue struggling, rising from the depths, but a blue dying, on the verge of gray, returning to the canyon floor. Snow fell, not heavily, but as soft swirling powder. Then the feeble sun came out, melting what it could, and descended beyond the rim.

After spending four days on the rim of the Grand Canyon, they left by train for Southern California. While Dolly loved its garden-like qualities, Zane had his eye on the sea and its fishing possibilities.

But California was not his present focus. For all his thirty-five years, he had been searching for something—what, he did not know. It was something intangible, something eternal, nourishing, and genuine. He had looked for it in his profession and not found it; he had sought it in his love life and writing career and not found it. But now and in the following few years, as he moved deeply into the high deserts of Arizona and Utah, he began to comprehend the dim outlines of what he had been seeking. Ultimately, the question he needed to answer was: "Who am I?"

*   *   *

A little over a year into the Greys' marriage, Zane began to sense he was back on Grubstreet. In January 1907, snow fell in Lackawaxen for days on end, causing him to shovel a foot of snow off his front steps and veranda. The woods around were ghostly quiet. Below the house, the Delaware River cut its dark, solemn way amid the pristine banks of snow. In the evenings he and Dolly huddled before the fireplace.

His writing prospects were as dismal as the weather. *Betty Zane* and *The Spirit of the Border*, on the whole, had received positive reviews. They had sold modestly but not enough to allow him to claim he was a successful author. *Field and Stream* continued to consider his outdoor and fishing articles.

In early February he took the three-hour train ride into New York City to attend a Campfire Club lecture featuring Charles Jesse "Buffalo" Jones and his exploits. Although born in Illinois, Jones made his hunting reputation in West Texas and New Mexico, where he partnered for a brief time with lawman Pat Garrett. Later he was appointed game warden of Yellowstone National Park by President Theodore Roosevelt. His latest venture was crossbreeding cattle with buffalo in hopes of producing "beefalo," sometimes called "cattalo," on his ranch on the North Rim of the Grand Canyon. Jones's storied career and derring-do adventures attracted a large audience that night. But some in the crowd found his brawny tales too unbelievable and hooted and howled their disapproval. Shaken, Jones retreated offstage.

It was there that an opportunistic writer met a distressed but unsung hero of a Wild West slowly disappearing into the dust of progress. Grey had the idea—something Jones later agreed to—that he would accompany the aging plainsman to his ranch in Arizona, where Grey would write about Jones's venture in a book. Grey made the offer to Buffalo Jones without first getting Dolly's consent, a move that produced endless guilt in the author. To finance the trip Grey would have to spend the remaining money from Dolly's inheritance. He returned to Lackawaxen and sheepishly told Dolly of his plans. Surprisingly, she agreed to the deal.

As her husband left for Arizona, she probably knew that Zane would never be the perfect nine-to-five career man and breadwinner, and that she would always have to take second place to the remote objects of his wanderlust. He once told her, "I need this wild life, this freedom."[1]

By the end of March, Grey was on the Santa Fe railroad heading southwest toward Albuquerque. "I am positively quivering with joy at the prospect of the trip," he wrote Dolly. He added that his depression had lifted and that he would come back to her loving her more than ever. In New Mexico, Grey changed into his "tough clothes," a heavy wool shirt, durable trousers, boots, bandana, and a slouch hat he had purchased at Wanamaker's before he left.[2]

After staying at the Alvarado Hotel, he boarded the train headed for Flagstaff via Gallup, Window Rock, Winslow, and Two Guns, Arizona. Although he knew he was going to see the real Arizona arid lands, he was also aware that the great wild spaces of the West were melting away like snowdrifts in June. The rattle and whistle of the train would soon drown out the shriek of the raven and the song of the meadowlark; the automobile would cover the traces of the painted ponies and the soft tread of the Hopi and Navajo hunters. He knew that he would have to find a niche in what remained of the Old West, but how it would take form was still beyond the horizon.

Arriving in Flagstaff, Grey steered toward the Weatherford Hotel, located a short block from the depot. The Weatherford was the appointed rendezvous point for Buffalo Jones and a party of Mormons who would soon join them. From there the group would head north, ford the Colorado River at Lee's Ferry, and head for Jones's ranch on the Kaibab Plateau. They hoped to accomplish the 250-mile journey by horse and pack mule, attended by some rowdy dogs.

First erected in 1896 but built of brick in 1900, the Weatherford boasted a three-story hotel plus a large saloon on the ground floor where travelers of the rail and the road gathered to swap their yarns. Over the course of his career, Grey came to love the Weatherford Hotel, which probably contained more of his footprints than any other commercial structure in the western United States.

In early April he wrote Dolly: "You ought to see this crowd of Mormons I'm going with. If they aren't a tough bunch I never saw one. They all pack guns. But they're nice fellows."[3]

This "tough bunch" accompanying Grey and Jones included E. D. Woolley and Jim Simpson Emmett. Grey reconsidered his fascination for Buffalo Jones, calling him "a selfish, forgetful old fool. He doesn't know where he is half the time. . . . I wish I had you instead of him. To hell with trains and wild trips. I want to write out of my mind and heart."[4] Woolley held a prominent role in the settling of Kanab, Utah, located just across the Arizona territorial border. He and his two wives lived on a church-owned cattle ranch in Kanab, where he was president of the Kanab Stake of the Church of Jesus Christ of Latter-day Saints (LDS). He was eager to tell Zane about the struggles of the Mormon settlements in southern Utah, in hopes that the ambitious author might someday relate their stories to a dubious world. Grey, in the same April letter to Dolly, admitted,

"Mr. Woolley wants me to go to Kanab to study the Mormons." And then Grey scribbled a line that must have made Dolly grimace: "He has two families, and fifteen handsome unmarried girls. I guess I won't go. I really would be afraid of so many."[5]

Grey was also drawn to Jim Emmett, who had recently been acquitted in Flagstaff of cattle rustling. Emmett was a large man, "standing well over six feet," wrote Zane, "and his leonine build, ponderous shoulders, and great shaggy head and white beard gave an impression of great virility and dignity."[6] He was born in 1850 in a covered wagon on the Mormon trail to Utah. When he met Grey he was fifty-seven years old and had lived in numerous settlements in Dixie, Utah, before settling on a small farm near Lee's Ferry, Arizona, where he managed the river-crossing equipment. Of all his companions, Grey admitted, "he was the man who influenced me most." He taught Zane about bravery, about a love for the desert, an appreciation of animals, and about endurance in a harsh and forbidding land. Emmett was a loner, going without most of the things yearned for by other men and enduring "pain, pain, always some kind of pain."[7]

Emmett influenced Grey as a moral leader and not as one of the heroes Grey was to champion in his fiction. Emmett stood counter to the fiery religious dogmatists who became the writer's villains. The tall bearded man and his group were the first Mormons Grey had met and they would forever shape his views of their struggles in the desert. Zane would immortalize Emmett as the stoic frontiersman in his fourth standalone novel, *The Heritage of the Desert* (1910). After the novel was published, the author wrote confidently: "I have given to the world the Mormons in a new better light."[8]

After circling the base of the San Francisco Peaks, they dropped down into scaly ochre desert.

Grey was riding his first horse since leaving Ohio and he groaned as his mount often stumbled on a rise in the ground. He became used to the routine of camp at twilight and slipping into his bedroll at night to behold a rain of stars. The Mormons rose first in the morning, started a fire, began saddling their horses, and checked the straps on their pack mules. "The morning came gray and cheerless," the author remarked. "I got up stiff and sore, with a tongue like a rope."[9]

They stayed west of the border of the Navajo Nation, intending to cross the Little Colorado and to head straight for Lee's Ferry on the big Colorado River. The confluence of the Little Colorado and the Colorado River to the west was held sacred by the Navajos. They referred to it as the "axis mundi," or the connection between heaven and earth. Jones and Emmett, however, cared little for native traditions or, for that matter, Native Americans in general. They openly hated Indians, a fact that disturbed Grey. He came to love and respect the Navajo, Hopi, and Paiute denizens of this region of the country. He particularly admired their tracking skills, stealth on the trail, and ability to know every inert and living thing in the desert from the dust to the stars.

Grey made notes along the route of the desert fauna and flora, pausing to ask Jones the names of certain trees and vegetation. Four-legged wild animals were scarce, but hawks and falcons circled over decaying prey far to their east. After encountering a bank of cedar and sagebrush, Grey heard the bleat of an animal. "I searched, and presently I found a little black and white lamb, scarcely able to stand. It came readily to me, and I carried it to the wagon."

"That's a Navajo lamb," said Emmett. "There are Navajo Indians close by."

Jones and the Mormons searched the horizon but saw no one. They plodded on under a glazed lemon sky, hoping to make Lee's Ferry by the fifth day of their trek.

The landscape fascinated Grey. "Imagination had pictured the desert for me a vast sandy plain, flat and monotonous. Reality showed me desolate mountains gleaming bare in the sun, long lines of red bluffs, and hills of blue clay . . . Thin, clear, sweet, dry, the desert air carried a languor, a dreaminess, tidings of far off things, and an enthralling promise. The fragrance of flowers, the beauty and grace of women, the sweetness of music, and the mystery of life—all seemed to float on that promise."

But Grey discovered the desert quickly makes a realist out of a romantic. He cried out to Emmett: "Look! Here are a red lake and trees!"

"No, lad, not a lake; it's what haunts the desert traveler. It's only a mirage."

Slightly embarrassed by his Midwestern naiveté, Grey chuckled to himself. "So I awoke to the realization of that illusive thing, a mirage, a beautiful lie, false as stairs of sand. . . . For a long moment it lay there, smiling in the sun, a thing almost intangible, and then it faded. I felt a sense of actual loss. So real had been the illusion that I could not believe I was not soon to drink and wade and dabble in the cool waters. Disappointment was keen."[10]

The next day the wind picked up and the blowing sand stung their faces. The joy they felt at the beginning of their trip vanished. Dust devils whirled and spun out of sight. That afternoon they encountered a sandstorm. "The Mormons covered themselves," noted Grey. "I wrapped a blanket round my head and hid behind a sage bush."[11] For several minutes the party sheltered where they stood. The wind roared and the sand seeped into their mouths and clothing. Grey peeped out periodically from a corner of his blanket. The fury of the storm passed; they waited until the sand stopped shifting and drifting. Ahead of them the trail was covered and the wagon wheels were hub-deep in the dust.

That evening the Mormons stopped their customary singing. Jones leaned back on his pack and took out a crude pipe with a long stem. He packed the bowl firm with a pinch of aromatic tobacco and lit it with a branch from the fire. After some manful sucking on the stem, he blew a stream of smoke into the night air and, contented, said nothing. Zane jotted some notes in his logbook. "The dogs were as limp as rags," wrote Grey.[12]

The next day, skirting the Vermillion Cliffs on their left, they soon heard the roar and whine of the Colorado River. Upstream the party came in sight of Lee's Ferry, where just across the river stood Emmett's place. Before there was a bridge across the Colorado and prior to the building of the Glen Canyon Dam to control water flow, the only way across the river was at Lee's Ferry. All land traffic traveling between northern Arizona and southwestern Utah had to pass using the ancient fording contraption at the ferry point. Named for Mormon elder John D. Lee, whose farm

Emmett took over, it was a focal point for much of the LDS migration out of southern Utah.*

When Zane saw the flimsy old scow he was to cross in, he shuddered. "I felt that I would rather start back alone over the desert than trust myself in such a craft, on such a river," he admitted. "And it was all because I had had experiences with bad rivers, and thought I was a judge of dangerous currents. The Colorado slid with a menacing roar out of a giant split in the red wall, and whirled, eddied, bulged on toward its confinement in the iron-ribbed canyon below."[13]

Presently Emmett fired two rifle shots into the air. In answer to the shots, two of Emmett's men on the opposite bank began rowing the craft toward Jones's group waiting patiently on the shoreline. After the craft arrived in front of Emmett and Jones, Grey and some of the men got in, the skiff wobbling and nodding in the current. Grey turned to Emmett and asked if he was a good swimmer. Emmett confessed he couldn't "swim a stroke." But Emmett added it didn't matter because "once in there a man's a goner. . . . We only drowned two men last year."

"Didn't you attempt to rescue them?" asked Grey.

"No use. They never came up."[14]

Toward dusk the remainder of the party and all the animals made it across the turbulent Colorado River. Grey watched from the shore in front of Emmett's thumbnail stretch of land.

Grey's safe perch offered him no comfort: "And all the time in my ears dinned the roar, the boom, the rumble of this singularly rapacious and purposeful river—a river of silt, a red river of dark, sinister meaning, a river with terrible work to perform, a river which never gave up its dead."[15]

* * *

Grey's views of Mormonism had been shaped by years of cultural bias that had opposed the church's teachings. But his brief sojourn with Emmett changed many of them. In Jim Emmett, Grey saw the best aspects of Mormon life in the West. Their ability to endure in this naked wilderness

---

* John Lee's contribution to the shaping of *Riders of the Purple Sage* will be discussed in the next chapter.

combined with their love of God produced a fascination for the novelist that remained with him all his life. Emmett's compassion stretched "to the outcast and the starved Indian; to wanderers of the wasteland who wandered by the ferry; to cowboys and sheepherders out of jobs. His gate was ever open. Rustlers and horse thieves, outlaws from the noted Hole in the Wall, hunted fugitives, were all welcomed by Jim Emmett. He had no fear of any man. He feared only his God."[16]

The desert provided Grey with ample features from which to hone his descriptive skills. Coming from the wooded sections of the East Coast, he was used to dense, impenetrable forests. But in the sharp, dry desert atmosphere, where one could see for a hundred miles, he began eyeing features with clarity and distinction. Mesas gained majesty; salmon- and buff-colored rock spurs rose boldly against the blue sky; the shifting sands heaved and flattened toward the faraway mountain peaks; and whole earth seemed to breathe and reveal its secrets to him. In this terrain the figure of a man seemed grander and more imposing; horse and rider appeared magisterial when advancing against the afternoon sun.

Grey's mind roamed. Could morality and duty be this clear and distinct? Could the men and women of the desert live peacefully here? Grey found that the desert magnified the good and evil qualities in men. Evil men became lawless; good men were ennobled. The civilizations of the desert developed their own moral laws. For the Mormons who lived here, religion and faith helped establish their own code of life. But Grey recognized that any dogma or fanatical adherence to a set of principles could quickly infect any placid setting. Any belief that clouded men's reasoning powers was suspect in Grey's view.

Ultimately, Grey found in men like Jim Emmett survivors who had endured the toils of wilderness—and prevailed. The author's highest accolade for any man went to him who had conquered the mountain, forded the river, and finished the race. It was not good enough to start a venture—one had to end it successfully. This became the test of all Grey's male characters.

* * *

Minus Emmett and his Mormon bunch, Buffalo Jones and Grey headed for Jones's ranch on the Kaibab (Paiute for "mountain lying down") Plateau. They headed southwest, and then turned due west, passing the Vermillion Cliffs on their right. A short distance up the trail, Zane looked up and saw the faint outlines of the low, wooded mountains of the plateau "covered with patches of shining snow. I could follow the zigzag line of the Grand Canyon splitting the desert plateau, and saw it disappear beyond the haze round the end of a mountain. From this I got my first clear impression of the topography of the country surrounding our objective point."[17] Approaches to the nearby Grand Canyon were fissured with box, slot, and forested canyons, surmounted by red sandstone spires and pillars.

With Jones in the lead and Grey riding a fresh mount, they plodded along, slowly ascending the slopes of the plateau. Two days later, after negotiating ridges and arroyos, they arrived at the ranch. Grey dismounted and limped into Jones's front room, where he settled his bones into an overstuffed, blanket-draped chair. Meanwhile, Jones counted his newborn calves.

"Twenty calves this spring!" Jones yelled. "Ten thousand dollars' worth of calves!"

Grey wished to share in Jones's triumph, but his body remained buried in the chair.

Ten days after leaving Flagstaff and trudging through northern Arizona, Grey was certain he could never lay claim to being a cowboy. In truth, he did not like to ride that much.[18]

They were soon joined by Grant Wallace, an amateur archeologist and explorer, who had been trailing them since leaving Flagstaff. Wallace brushed off his coat, sending a fine powder of dust into the air. "I've been on your trail for twelve days," said Wallace. He explained that he nearly caught up to them at the Little Colorado, but was delayed crossing Lee's Ferry. Grey clasped Wallace's hand. "The hounds sniffed around Wallace," Grey added, "and welcomed him with vigorous tails."[19]

Two days later, Frank, one of Jones's wranglers, picked out a strong mustang for Grey to ride.

"Of course you can ride?" asked Frank.

The Wupatki ruins just north of Flagstaff were one of Zane's first encounters with the Indian culture of the Southwest.

Since a greenhorn rarely admits his shortcomings, Grey smirked. After Frank saddled the mustang, Grey cautiously mounted it. Before he could grab the reins, the horse bolted forward, carrying a shocked author in the direction of Buffalo Jones riding up ahead. Clinging desperately to the saddle, Grey was finally able to rein in the mustang near Jones's horse.

"What in thunder did Frank give you that white nag for?' Jones bellowed. "The buffalo hate white horses—anything white. They're liable to stampede off the range, or chase you into the canyon."[20]

Grey shrugged his shoulders. By this time, he was prepared for any eventuality—tragic, comic, or otherwise.

* * *

The whole purpose of Grey's expedition with Buffalo Jones had been to record the hunter's experience with crossbreeding cattle with buffalo. But as time passed, the author realized the trip had become much more. What started out as a freshman course in the terrain of northern Arizona had become a graduate seminar in the West. Among his discoveries were the studies of cowboy lore and horses; the crafts and customs of the Navajo, Hopi, and Paiute Indians; the vegetation and animals of the high desert; and the sounds and odors of the canyon and mountain country. Near the Arizona-Utah border, the mesquite and juniper gave way to carpeted valleys of purple sage that after a rain smelled of camphor and licorice. The sage grew high, often near the belly of a horse. Yard upon yard, mile upon mile, the sage spread from meadows and filled the furrows of ridges and mesas. This stark and wonderful country needed a large vocabulary to express its unique qualities. He would return to the Southwest in 1908 and again in 1909, but this April 1907 journey through northern Arizona and southern Utah would supply a storehouse of knowledge that would ultimately influence his first two Western novels, *Heritage of the Desert* and *Riders of the Purple Sage*. The "purple sage" referred to in Grey's title for his second Western novel was without doubt the basin sage, or *Artemisia tridentata*, which grows in wild profusion throughout the plateaus and high deserts of the Southwest. It has silvery-green leaves, but daylight combined with atmospheric effects as the sagebrush recedes in the distance gives it a purple sheen. The sagebrush plant provides food for

Toadstool hoodoo in the Escalante National Monument, Utah

pronghorn and sage grouse but is toxic to humans. Containing roughly 40 percent camphor, basin sage is a staple in the Western landscape and a symbol for Zane Grey of the singular wildness of this rugged outback.

Grey's literary "rectangle" in these novels extended from the North Rim of the Grand Canyon east to Kayenta; north through Monument Valley to Monticello, Utah; due west, inclusive of the Rainbow Bridge and the Escalante Plateau, to Cedar City and Kanab. This rugged territory comprises Mormon and Gentile (non-Mormon) settlements, parts of the Navajo Nation, and the dominion of gold-seekers, adventurers, explorers, rustlers, outlaws, and wanderers of the wasteland.

At Snake Gulch, a short distance west of Jacob Lake, Arizona, they stumbled upon Grey's first glimpse of Indian rock art. The gulch floor was filled with patches of bristly sagebrush, and the gravel benches made footing difficult. Zane, Wallace, and Jones clambered up a rock face to study the figures. Grey reached out a hand, stroking the rock wall.

"The figure was a dark, red devil," he reported, "a painted image, rude, unspeakably wild, crudely executed but painted by the hand of man. The whole surface of the cliff wall bore figures of all shapes—men, animals, birds, and strange devices, some in red paint, mostly in yellow. Some showed the wear of time; others were clear and sharp."[21]

Jones caught his breath. "Darn me if I ever saw an animal like that! Boys, this is a find, sure as you're born. Because not even the Paiutes spoke of these figures. I doubt if they even know they're here. And the cowboys and the wranglers, what few ever get by here in a hundred years, never saw these things. Beats anything I ever saw on the Mackenzie, or anywhere else."[22]

Grey continued his reporting: "There was a character representing a great chief, before whom many figures lay prostrate, evidently slain or subjugated. Large red paintings, in the shape of bats, occupied prominent positions, and must have represented gods or devils. Armies of marching men told of that blight of nation's old or young—war. These, and birds unnamable, and beasts unclassable, with dots and marks and hieroglyphs, recorded the history of a bygone people. Symbols they were of an era that had gone into the dim past, leaving only these marks, forever unintelligible . . . reminders of the glory, the mystery, the sadness of life."

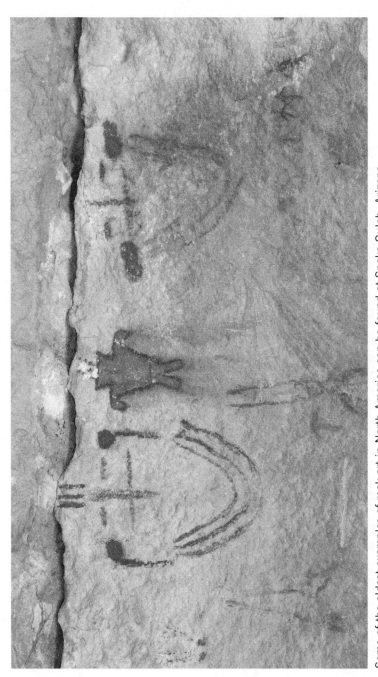

Some of the oldest examples of rock art in North America can be found at Snake Gulch, Arizona.
WORKING TITLE PRODUCTIONS @SHUTTERSTOCK.COM

Jones was stunned. "How could paint of any kind last so long?"

"That is the unsolvable mystery," said Wallace. "But the records are there. I am absolutely sure the paintings are at least a thousand years old. I have never seen any tombs or paintings similar to them. Snake Gulch is a find, and I shall someday study its wonders."[23] (Contemporary scientific studies have dated the paintings between 500 BC and 1150 AD. The paintings are one of the largest concentrations of pictographs in North America.)

They climbed down from the cracked, scarred Coconino sandstone rocks and mounted their horses. As Grey's sojourn was drawing to a close, the author told Jones that he would soon begin writing his book. When it was complete, he would invite Jones to Lackawaxen and have him review it before publication. Zane had made notes throughout the trip, so now it was a process of turning his scribblings into a compelling narrative.

After weeks in the dry air of Arizona, Grey's skin felt like paper. He had saddle sores and his joints ached. Jones told him he now had the stealth and desert skills of a Navajo brave.

Next to Dolly telling him he had the makings of great writer, it was the best compliment he had ever received.

CHAPTER FOUR

The Reckoning

AFTER LEAVING JONES'S RANCH, GREY TOOK THE SHORTCUT ROUTE. HE headed south across the North Rim of the Grand Canyon, and then ferried across the Colorado River to a point below El Tovar Hotel, where he assembled his notes of the trip. On board the Santa Fe back to Pennsylvania, he began chronicling his experiences. He wrote quickly, hardly stopping to eat or leave the train to stretch his legs.

His memoir featured Buffalo Jones and Jim Emmett in the central roles as plainsman and Mormon patriarch, respectively. Covering the highlights of his trip from Flagstaff to northern Arizona, the book became his obsession for the next five months. Crossing out several working titles, he finally settled on *The Last of the Plainsmen*. As the train sped eastward, he had only one goal: to finish the book and get it published, preferably by Harper and Brothers.

It was fortunate that Jones knew Ripley Hitchcock, the senior editor at Harper. Jones had arranged a meeting with Hitchcock for Grey to pitch his book when it was completed. The knowledge that he would have a sympathetic ear at Harper encouraged him through the writing process.

At home in Lackawaxen, Grey found the maples and oaks in full bloom; fresh from the grips of winter, the Delaware glided lazily down the grassy banks. He went straight to work at his desk. Sharpening a handful of pencils, he poured out his narrative, weeding out deadwood, revising common clichés, and focusing his attention on creating concrete nouns and action verbs. Most of the book flowed easily, and he realized that he must keep the rhythm and pace of the book constantly moving forward.

Dolly read his drafts and began tightening the narrative. Both Grey and his wife wanted the story to move swiftly from sequence to sequence. The focus would shift from the desert trek to Emmett's farm and Jones's ranch. Dolly penciled out extraneous narrative and sharpened the most important scenes.

The result was a fast-paced, exciting, and readable narrative, spliced with vivid descriptions of northern Arizona Territory. Because it was not a fictional account, Buffalo Jones, Jim Emmett, and Grant Wallace retained their true names in the manuscript.

Grey soon wrote Jones that the book was ready for his review. Jones arrived in the waning months of 1907 and proceeded to park himself in a comfy chair with Zane's manuscript. From his chuckles and dead silences, Grey sensed that the old hunter liked the book. When Jones proclaimed it the best book he had ever read on the subject, the author beamed.

Jones had arranged a meeting time with Ripley Hitchcock, and so the duo, Grey toting his manuscript, headed to New York. Jones wore his faded buckskin jacket with beads down the sleeves while Grey looked spruced up in his coat and tie. Overlooking Franklin Square, the Harper and Brothers structure added a distinct architectural profile to the Manhattan skyline. The building featured wrought iron columns and supporting trusses; below the Harper sign at the top of the façade were statues of Washington, Jefferson, and Franklin. The building's size and details were meant to impress if not overwhelm the viewer.

The interior employed a spiral staircase, with each step buttressed by iron supports. Often called "the steps to fame," they had conveyed such luminaries as Herman Melville, Henry James, Mark Twain, Owen Wister, Richard Harding Davis, Winslow Homer, and Frederic Remington.

Grey and Jones slowly made their way upstairs to the editorial offices and paced in the lobby.

Ripley Hitchcock was indeed the man to see. As head of the literary department, he could lift or crush a writer's ambitions. If he rejected a writer's work, it was dropped by Harper. If another opinion was needed, he sent the manuscript up to his boss, Frederick Duneka, the general manager of operations.

Hitchcock was busy at his desk on the third floor when Zane Grey and Buffalo Jones came through the door. The editor recognized the burly-shouldered hunter. Momentarily Hitchcock sized up Grey. He saw a man of average height and rugged build. His cheekbones were reddened by the sun and wind, and his dark, coarse hair seemed combed by his hand; his mouth and lips were resolute, and his eyes shone with great expectations.

They shook hands, and Grey handed the editor the manuscript. Hitchcock was genial, telling them both that it certainly looked like a property that Harper could publish. However, said Hitchcock, he would take a few days to read it and allow his in-house readers to consider it as well. The editor said he would report back in a couple of weeks.

Presently, Grey and Jones left Harper and headed to Grand Central Terminal, where Jones took the train back to Arizona and Grey returned to Lackawaxen.

A short while later Dolly brought Zane a letter from Hitchcock, telling him he'd like to see Grey in his office. Once in Hitchcock's presence, Grey's normally placid expression turned somber. Hitchcock held Grey's manuscript. "I've read this and some of the people in the office have gone through it," the editor said gravely. "I'm sorry to have to tell you that the decision is that we should not publish it." Hitchcock handed him the manuscript and said: "I do not see anything in this to convince me you can write either narrative or fiction." Hitchcock added that he found Grey's work "vain, fine, personal, overwritten, and too full of adjectives."[1]

Grey didn't wait for any more salvos to head his way. Shocked, he cradled the manuscript and headed out the door and down the circular stairs. Once on Franklin Square he tried to make sense of what he had just heard. When he got to Grand Central Terminal, he finally realized that Harper had, for the fourth time, rejected his work. On this occasion, however, an editor—the senior editor—had the audacity to do it in person.

On the train to Lackawaxen, his heart felt "like a squeezed orange." Complicating his mood was the idea of having to tell Dolly. He prepared himself for the prospect of having to return to dentistry to make ends meet. His idea to become a writer nearly ten years ago seemed pathetically foolish.

But by the time he reached the depot at Lackawaxen, his mood had brightened. "Suddenly something marvelous happened to me, in my mind, to my eyesight, to my breast. That moment should logically have been the end of my literary aspirations. From every point of view I seemed lost. But someone inside me cried out: 'He does not know. They are all wrong.'"[2]

His rise from the ashes was affirmed by Dolly, who again supported his decision to keep writing. If Grey sustained the courage to remain a writer in those dark years, a good deal of the credit goes to Dolly, who by some inherent belief kept her husband on course. Winter set in, a frigid one even by the standards of northeastern Pennsylvania. Grey mailed out *The Last of the Plainsmen* to Macmillan, who he believed would provide a receptive audience to his project.

A short time later he approached the Outing Publishing Company, a minor publishing firm but reputable enough for critics and readers to pay attention to the book.

* * *

Throughout his career, Zane Grey was always perplexed by Harper and Brothers' decision to reject his work. He was especially angered by Ripley Hitchcock's reaction to his first work on the West. What did Hitchcock mean by saying he could not write "either narrative or fiction"?

It would have helped immensely if Hitchcock had explained Harper's position further, but, alas, all attempts at being rational were dashed in a moment of soul murder. Ripley Hitchcock was much more than a bookish, bespectacled, comma-hunting old fogey hired by telegram to appease great writers and torment beginning ones. At fifty years of age in 1907, he was probably among the most accomplished editors in New York. After graduating from Harvard in 1877, he became a successful journalist and art critic at the *New-York Tribune* in 1882. In 1890 he became an advisor at the D. Appleton Publishing Company. In this role he was able to encourage editors within the company to publish important new writers.

As early as 1892 he took a talented novice under his wing named Stephen Crane. Hitchcock recognized in Crane a realistic voice crying, as it were, from the Bowery and the Civil War battlefields of America. Hitchcock also knew that Crane's writing was so original, gritty, and spot-on that it might threaten its commercial value. The two worked closely on editing Crane's first novel, *Maggie*, with Hitchcock eliminating most of the objectionable material. In a later edition, Hitchcock urged Crane to strike out "a goodly number of damns and words which hurt." While *Maggie* was selling well and circulating in the populace, Crane appeared in Hitchcock's office with his new novel, *The Red Badge of Courage*. Recognizing raw but brilliant material when he saw it, Hitchcock labored on making *The Red Badge* as saleable as possible.

Both Hitchcock and Crane were fierce opponents of romanticism in literature. Although Crane died in 1900, five years after the publication of *The Red Badge of Courage*, his influence later on the school of realism was profound. Jack London, Theodore Dreiser, Sinclair Lewis, and Willa Cather, among many others, came under his spell.

Thus, when Ripley Hitchcock encountered the work of Zane Grey, he was unprepared at the time to appreciate it. He had been at Harper and Brothers since 1906, barely a year before meeting Grey. His role was to scout, approve, and edit the work of the most talented writers in the world. He was also a competent historian, having written two books on the West: *The Lewis and Clark Expedition* (1905) and *The Louisiana Purchase* (1903). Hitchcock was probably the best person in a position to recognize the talent of Zane Grey. So, why didn't he?

The answer perhaps lies in a set of guidelines popular among publishers at the beginning of the twentieth century. For Harper to accept a book for publication, three conditions had to be met: (1) The book should have intrinsic literary merit; (2) the author should have enough stature so that his name helps sell and promote the book; and (3) the book should fit somewhere in the list of categories outlined by the publisher.

To arrive at a publishing decision, Hitchcock trusted not only his own inner voice, but also the opinions of his two in-house readers, William Briggs, of the *New York Journal*, and William Bucklin Wells, who also served as an editor of *Harper's* magazine. All three seemed to agree that Grey had met condition number one, although Briggs pointed out that Grey's style was average but still acceptable. *The Last of the Plainsmen* was fairly well-written, unique, and well-paced, with a strong and, at times, humorous authorial voice. It was not a biography of Buffalo Jones in the traditional sense, but a brief, insightful glimpse into his life in northern Arizona. Hitchcock and his readers considered it more of a memoir than a work of fiction.

The book also met the third condition. Harper's list was quite extensive, ranging from books on art and architecture to Western history and biographies of notable people. Buffalo Jones would have made an interesting cradle-to-grave biography, but Grey decided that he was not a trained biographer. In the place of a formal biographical treatment, he opted for a personalized, first-person account of Jones's experiences near the North Rim of the Grand Canyon. Both Hitchcock and his readers had no issue with Grey's approach. As a matter of fact, they liked his rollicking adventure story.

But the important second condition was not met. In 1904 Harper published *The Adventures of Buffalo Bill* by William F. Cody, a freewheeling account of his escapades in the West. Although it was not a best seller, it gave Harper some eminence in the Western story. The book was followed in 1906 by Rex Beach's *The Spoilers*, a top-selling saga, not a Western exactly, but a "Northwestern" of life in the Klondike and Alaska. In 1907, the unsung Zane Grey simply did not have the platform to help make *The Last of the Plainsmen* a commercial success.

After Harper's rejection of the book, it was turned down by eleven other publishers before being accepted in early 1908 by Outing Publishing.

The string of rejections made Grey even more resentful of the publishing world. "I do not like the inside workings of a publishing house," he noted in his diary. "I am beginning to see, to learn things I have never dreamed of before. The men connected with publishing houses have their interests the same as any other men. . . . They care absolutely nothing about being true to human life. [Briggs] makes light of the deeper purpose in literature. I believe he thinks he has discovered a number of young writers, and imagines he controls them, or directs their efforts, and takes complacent credit for it."[3]

But Ripley Hitchcock remained his greatest literary nemesis. Grey called him "a sophisticated, conventional, cultured mossback. . . . To the

A saddled horse rests in Navajo Country in a setting similar to that of John Wetherill's trading post at Kayenta.

young writer he is patronizing, suave, condescending, and superior. He expects to be looked up to. He will likely suggest changes to everything the young writer does, not because the work needs it, but because he must be felt. I suppose he has to fight to hold his job the same way I have to fight to find a publisher. Still it is the most damnable attitude I've yet to stand."[4]

As Zane continued to smolder about his treatment from the publisher, he turned his attention once again to the Western landscape.

In 1908 several explorations were afoot to excavate some of the remote landmarks in the American Southwest. Many of these sites had been the ancestral home of Pueblo Indians. One of the most important expeditions was directed by Byron Cummings, a University of Utah archeologist, and William Douglas, an examiner of surveys for the US government. Cummings and Douglas, who frequently argued over who should have the first glimpse of a site, hired John Wetherill, the famed explorer and trader. John and his wife, Louisa, ran the trading post at Kayenta, Arizona, and were frequently consulted on excavations in the desert.

Although both Cummings and Douglas wanted first views of the legendary Rainbow Bridge in southern Utah, they combined forces and agreed to share the experience. Guided by Wetherill and a Ute Indian named Jim Mike, they left Kayenta and headed over the massive Navajo Mountain into Utah. Along the way they were joined by the Paiute Nasja Begay, who added his expertise in desert navigation.

In mid-summer 1908, they finally reached Rainbow Bridge and became the first Anglo explorers to gaze upon its remarkable 275-foot span over the gulch. Five years later it would draw Zane Grey, who would come in search of the Rainbow Trail, and former president Theodore Roosevelt, who simply wanted to marvel at its beauty.

In the same year, Grey was searching for treasures of another sort. R. C. had lent Zane $100 to rendezvous with Buffalo Jones and Jim Emmett on the North Rim, on a journey he described vividly in "Roping Lions in the Grand Canyon" (*Field and Stream*, January 1909). Grey was receiving a modest amount from his magazine articles, which sustained him during the desperate years.

On this particular trip he also managed to visit E. D. Woolley of Kanab, Utah, the Mormon who had accompanied him from Flagstaff to Emmett's farm the previous year.

With a population of over seven hundred, Kanab (Paiute for "willows"), along with St. George and Cedar City, were Mormon strongholds in Utah's Dixie. But due to its geography and location, Kanab seemed a territory unto itself. St. George and Cedar City were positioned on the trail from Salt Lake City to California, while Kanab was fringed in stands of verdant cottonwoods and lay sprawled in the shadows of the high, red-tinged buttes. Industrious farmers worked the land, hoping to stave off plagues of grasshoppers. On the outskirts of town several ranches raised cattle and sheep.

Arriving in Kanab, Grey felt welcomed by his Mormon hosts. Men in long dark jackets and women in dresses and sunbonnets milled about along Main Street. Minus saloons, cafes, and ramshackle hotels, the hamlet looked surprisingly tidy. Little Italianate homes with gables and picket fences lined the streets radiating from the main thoroughfare.

Grey met Mr. Woolley at the guesthouse run by Thomas Cole. Here Grey would spend a few nights learning of the local and regional history. On these sojourns in the West, Grey was much more of an eager student than he was in his Penn days.

Edwin Dilworth Woolley was stake president of Kanab. Called "Uncle Woolley" or sometimes "Wild and Woolley," Edwin was both the political and spiritual leader of Kanab. A gregarious and vocal sixty-three year old, Woolley fascinated Grey with his stories of Kanab's and southern Utah's pioneer history. Woolley and his son–in–law, Dave Rust, helped Zane connect the lives of Jim Emmett with those of the Mormon settlers in Utah. The results of such an encounter would find their way into Zane's breakout Western novels.

It was a well-known fact around Kanab that Woolley was an eccentric visionary who had a plan, among other ideas, to build a road all the way to the North Rim of the Grand Canyon. The road, stretching about eighty miles between the two points, would be suitable for a modern roadster and horse-drawn vehicles. Woolley and Rust envisioned a byway that would draw tourists and locals, creating a bonanza for southern Utah and boosting the morale of the town citizens. Woolley planned his project for the following year, and with the help of his son-in-law, a mule train, and a work crew, he believed he could complete the road in a year.

Grey recognized a shrewd method in Woolley's madness. A trail to the North Rim would add a new dimension to Grand Canyon travel. While the Santa Fe Railroad provided a comfortable ride from Williams, Arizona, to the South Rim of the canyon, Woolley's project would open a whole new way to see one of the natural wonders of the world. It would have to cut through sagebrush, piñon, and juniper and navigate jagged rocks on its course southward, but the benefits far outweighed the drawbacks.

*   *   *

During his brief stay in Kanab and purple sage country, Grey acquired a deeper understanding of the area and the men and women who pioneered it. Several names came to the forefront, including Levi Stewart, who founded the town in 1870, and John D. Lee. Lee spent a brief time in Kanab, then moved on to Mountain Meadows, to Harmony, and finally to Lee's Ferry, Arizona, the site on the Colorado River that bears his name. Lee's fiery nature, rugged features, and explosive personality attracted Grey. The Mormon villains in Grey's most famous novel are based on the enigmatic character of John Doyle Lee.

Lee was born in Illinois in 1812 and joined the Mormon Church when he was twenty-six.

He became close to Brigham Young, who by an early church doctrine adopted Lee as his son.

Persecuted and tormented by angry mobs, the Mormon followers in Missouri and Illinois withdrew into a walled fortress, a move that hardened their resolve and promoted their distrust of the government and outsiders. During this time Lee received blessings from the church elders, one of whom declared that he "would have power over his enemies. And understand the hidden things of heaven." Lee pledged to "pray and never cease to pray, and never cease to importune high heaven to avenge the blood of the prophets on this nation." Brigham Young told him: "I have unsheathed my sword, and will never return it until the blood of the prophet Joseph and Hyrum, and those who were slain in Missouri, is avenged." John Lee promised "to avenge the blood of the prophet whenever the opportunity offered."[5]

Lee could quickly turn vengeful. In 1845 he was betrothed to a young woman named Emmeline. One day Brigham Young saw her and fell in love with her. Young coerced Lee into surrendering Emmeline to him, promising Lee that he would sit at Young's right hand in his kingdom. The request tormented Lee, and reluctantly he gave her up to the most powerful leader in the Mormon Church. Among Young's many wives, Emmeline became one of his favorites, bearing him ten children. Over the years, Lee raged at how Young had manipulated him.

After the great migration west in 1847 and the settling of the Salt Lake Valley, Mormon followers began colonizing other parts of the territory. Towns and villages sprang up north and south of the Salt Lake and along the benches of the Wasatch Mountains, spreading farther south and west along a corridor that led to California. Cedar City and St. George bloomed out of this growth process.

By 1857 Brigham Young had solidified his formidable grip on the Mormon Church and its believers. In Washington, President James Buchanan became concerned that Utah Territory might develop into a sovereign state, which would threaten the jurisdiction of the US government and impede the flow of commerce to the western states. He deployed the US Army to Utah, which inflamed President Brigham Young and forced him into forming militia groups throughout the territory to block the army's advance. More of a guerrilla movement than an organized resistance body, the Mormon settlers planned various methods of thwarting the US Army.

At the height of the standoff, in September 1857, John Lee stood shoulder to shoulder with members of his militia group in southern Utah. For weapons they used farm tools such as scythes, hoes, and pitchforks. The fire in their bellies was stoked by years of oppression in Missouri and a raging desire to avenge the blood of the prophets. At the root of all their behavior was paranoia, the paralyzing fear

After a bear hunt in Arizona, Zane posed with his quarry for this photograph.

born of isolation and the prospect of facing an enemy—if indeed it was an enemy.

But presently they faced another threat. Lee and his militia group working near Cedar City learned of a party of emigrants approaching from the north on their way to California. The Fancher party consisted of 120 men, women, and children. Rumor spread around the Mormon militia that certain members of the party had taken part in the murder of prophets Joseph Smith and his brother Hyrum. Leaders of the Mormons worried that if they let the Fancher party proceed, they might encourage an army from California to attack. At first Lee voted to let them pass, but he was outvoted by the other leaders. Messengers traveled back and forth between Cedar City and Salt Lake City, bringing fresh dispatches from the church authorities. After furious debate among the Mormon leaders on the scene, John Higbee, a major in the Iron County Militia, proclaimed to the other leaders: "Have not these people threatened to murder our leaders and Prophet, and have they not boasted of murdering our Patriarchs and Prophets, Joseph and Hyrum? . . . Why brethren, there is not a drop of innocent blood in that entire camp of Gentile outlaws; they are a set of cutthroats, robbers, and assassins . . . who aided to shed the blood of our Prophets, Joseph and Hyrum, and it is our orders from all in authority, to get the emigrants from their stronghold, and help the Indians kill them."[6] The mercurial Lee at last stepped forward and agreed with Higbee. "It is a duty we owe to God," Lee announced, "and to our church and people. The orders from those in authority are that all the emigrants must die."[7]

Fueled by vengeance, fear and bloodlust, the Mormon militia prepared to act. They enlisted the help of Paiute Indians to help in their plan. The once equivocal John Lee became instrumental in the attack. The siege of the Fancher wagon party began on September 7 and ended on September 11, 1857, in Mountain Meadows, located between Cedar City and St. George. Some Mormons were dressed as Indians, so that later they could blame the Paiutes for the massacre. Some in the emigrant party resisted the onslaught of gunshots, rifle butts, and sabers. Most of the Fancher group was ruthlessly cut down, but seventeen children under the age of six were spared. John Lee was in the middle of the deadly melee. One of the Paiutes recalled that Lee "was like a wild beast who had tasted fresh blood. He was turned into a demon."[8]

The survivors related lurid tales of indiscriminate savagery. Rebecca Dunlap recalled that "the Mormons shot down in cold blood the defenseless men, women, and children, then pierced them with bows and arrows, then cut their throats with knives." Another survivor, Sarah Baker, who was only three years old at the time, recalled later that the massacre started when she clung to her father. "You don't forget the horror," she claimed. "You don't forget the blood-curdling war whoops and the banging of guns all around you. You don't forget the screaming of other children and the agonized shrieks of women being hacked to death with tomahawks. And you won't forget it either when your own mother topples over in the wagon beside you, with a big red splotch getting bigger on the front of her calico dress."[9]

After the massacre and the disposal of the emigrants' bodies, Lee and the other leaders pledged to keep the secret from "the entire world. Not to tell their wives or most intimate friends."[10] Thus began the campaign among the Mormon offenders first to shift blame to the Indians and later to declare that they acted according to the will of a higher authority.

Several days after the incident at Mountain Meadows, John Lee stood in front of Brigham Young and related his version of the massacre. Young was troubled by the killing of women and children, but sought to find plausible ways the Mormon Church could be absolved of the crime. Lee maintained he and his men were only following orders, acting in "conformity with the oaths that they had all taken to avenge the blood of the prophets."[11] Most of the blame would rest on the shoulders of the Paiute Indians—until a federal investigation proved otherwise.

The ensuing months stretched into years. In 1861 the Civil War precluded any serious investigation into the massacre. John Lee retreated to his home in Harmony, Utah, where the citizens elected him as their presiding elder. An elder supervises the daily activities of the ward and may have the discretion to teach, baptize, exhort, and sometimes discipline members of the Mormon community found to be in violation of their doctrines and covenants.

The Mountain Meadows Massacre of 1857 became one of the most significant events in America's westward expansion. Colored lithograph.

Perhaps no man is more famous—or infamous—for his actions in the Mountain Meadows Massacre than John D. Lee.

As he entered his fifties, Lee continued to salve his conscience with the idea that he was merely following the dictates of the covenants. If this didn't work, he could blame the authority of the church for his misdeeds. He began to turn on Brigham Young, who behind the scenes was starting to incriminate Lee in the massacre. Townspeople thought Lee was making his religion a scapegoat for his actions.[12] As rumors persisted throughout southern Utah about Lee's involvement in the massacre, he continued to keep a low profile and welcome fellow Mormons to his house. He viewed Gentiles with suspicion or outright hatred.

As his guilt deepened, Lee's temper and behavior became more erratic. Over the years he had eighteen wives, eleven of whom deserted him for one reason or another. At any one time he would have eight or ten wives living with him. Most were in fear for their lives. John Lee prohibited anyone from speaking about the massacre in his home. When one of the surviving children of the incident disappeared, it was rumored that Lee had killed her and disposed of her body on his property. A neighbor called him "a swindler in dealing, a liar in conversation, and a low sensual brute of a man."[13] Several of Harmony's residents were wary of Lee's "brutal and immoral conduct of his home life."[14]

By the end of the 1860s, the Mormon Church felt pressure from the US government and from within its own ranks. There had been a warrant for Lee's arrest since 1859, but no one had expressed interest in serving it. In 1870 Brigham Young formally excommunicated Lee from the church and initiated plans for his adopted son to leave Utah. Young advised him to "trust no one. Make yourself scarce and keep out of the way."[15]

Feeling pressure from all sides, John Lee decided to accompany his lifelong friend Levi Stewart to the present site of Kanab, called by the Indians "Skutumpah." Stewart erected a sawmill and with assistance from fellow Mormons laid out the town. After a brief sojourn in Kanab, Lee headed across the border into Arizona Territory and cleared land near the crossing of the Colorado River, the crossing that became known as Lee's Ferry. He called it Lonely Dell—and it was: a forlorn, forgotten, hardscrabble speck of land surrounded by red earth and red cliffs and baked on certain ominous mornings by a red, angry sun. The surly Colorado roared

One of the major crossings of the Colorado River, Lee's Ferry still bears the legacy of John D. Lee and Jim Emmett.

out of a northern split in the rocks, chocolate brown and able to swallow anything in its path.

On November 7, 1874, Lee was arrested by United States marshal William Stokes and transported to Beaver, Utah, for his role in the Mountain Meadows Massacre. His first trial ended in a hung jury, but at his second trial in 1876 a jury found him guilty of first-degree murder. Lee was given the options of death by hanging, beheading, or firing squad. Hanging was not acceptable to Lee. Only cattle rustlers and bank robbers and other despicable vermin got hanged on a "hoss." Beheading, the preferred method of blood atonement, was also unacceptable, possibly because Lee wanted to keep his body intact. He ended up with death by firing squad, an agreeable method of dispatch that would offer some poetic justice to his victims at Mountain Meadows and provide him the opportunity to shed his blood for the prophets or anyone else that sought atonement.

His sentence was carried out on the afternoon of March 23, 1877, on the barren fields of Mountain Meadows. Even though the execution was supposedly kept secret, a crowd had gathered along with the members of the firing squad who were priming their Springfield rifles. A cold wind drifted down the valley as John Lee wedged his hat on top of his bristly hair and sat down on the edge of his coffin. He had engaged a local photographer and asked him to send a copy of his photo to his three faithful wives. After Lee muttered a few last words, the squad took their places. A brief volley of rifle fire crackled through the meadow. The figure slumped back in his coffin, his legs dangling over the side.

After the passing of John Lee, much of the dark stain of the massacre was removed. Some lamented his death while others thanked the heavens. Martyr or scapegoat, able lieutenant or sadistic killer—everyone had his opinion.

When Zane Grey needed an adversary evil enough to motivate his lead characters, he, too, had an opinion.

* * *

In the 1870s, Utah Territory saw a large influx of non-Mormons as well as Mormons from the east.

A Mormon settler sits in the doorway surrounded by his family, circa 1870.
EVERETT HISTORICAL @ SHUTTERSTOCK.COM

The Comstock Lode, the Pikes Peak gold strike, and the arrival of the transcontinental railroad heralded a new era in the life of the region. By 1880, non-Mormon owners of cattle ranches in southern Utah and northern Arizona started to expand their properties into territory previously run by Mormons. Battles for water rights ensued. Riders and triggermen threatened Mormon landowners in Verdure. Near Monticello, a band of riders known as the Carlisle cowboys regularly had skirmishes with Ute Indians and Mormon settlers. This lawless land was barely held in check by the owners of the cattle companies and the grudging goodwill of the Mormons.

In 1895, forty-five-year-old Jim Emmett took over operation of Lee's Ferry. Travelers paid him in cows, Navajo blankets, or trinkets. Within a short time, Emmett's herd of "scrub cows" had grown considerably, but the only place to graze them in winter was on land owned by the Grand Canyon Cattle Company, which went by the name Bar Z. The Bar Z ran one hundred thousand head of cattle throughout the Arizona Strip and directed their armed riders to trample the dreams of any small businessman, especially one upstart Mormon working from Lee's Ferry. The Bar Z erected a barbed wire fence along the border of its property. Emmett crashed the fence with a herd of buffalo followed by his small band of cattle. The dispute continued into the next decade and had each side toting guns wherever they went. Emmett journeyed to court in Flagstaff in 1907, where he pleaded not guilty to a charge of cattle rustling by the Bar Z. After the trial, Grey met him and was impressed by his stoic resistance to the gun-toting riders of the purple sage.

In the late spring of 1908, Grey left on the Santa Fe Railroad, bound for Chicago and Lackawaxen. At this time his idea for a Western novel was completely formless. Impressionistic memories flashed through his head: Mormon elders and cattle rustlers, riders of the range and towering vermillion buttes. The land, the people, and their conflicts were much the same as they had been thirty or forty years earlier, when the Old West truly was an era of color and excitement.

Maybe he wasn't too late after all.

Chapter Five

The House of Harper

Despite the fact that he had three works of adult fiction in print, Zane Grey didn't consider himself a serious novelist. The *Betty Zane* series of three books initially showed a poor return in proportion to the time and effort he had put into them. Only when he had a name did they begin to turn a profit.

There were a couple of hurdles he needed to overcome before he could turn to writing a novel of the West, a project he desperately wished to accomplish. The first was his mental barrier, which was largely shaped by public tastes and opinion. Could he be considered a serious novelist by writing a blood-and-thunder novel about the West?

The second hurdle, and the most serious one, concerned the words of Ripley Hitchcock—that Grey was incapable of penning a commercial work of fiction or narrative. Hitchcock's words seemed to haunt him everywhere he went, whether he was enjoying a cup of coffee in his Morris chair at home or walking absentmindedly down Madison Avenue in New York.

These worries nettled him all the way home from Arizona in the summer of 1908, and then, as if he had received manna from heaven, a notable shift occurred in his thinking. It came in a most unusual way: not from an editor or from Dolly, but from a book that a writer friend had recommended. The book was Clayton Hamilton's *Materials and Methods of Fiction*, published the same spring by Baker and Taylor. No single work can free an author to write his best book, but Hamilton's seminal work nudged Grey from a writer on the precipice to one who jumped into the flow of the river. Besides giving Grey confirmation of his own vision for a novel, it revolutionized his concepts of plot, character, and setting.

According to Loren Grey, Hamilton's work was "Father's bible. It had more influence on his work than any other book."[1]

Grammar books were plentiful in early twentieth-century America, but style and usage manuals were something of a rarity. The general feeling among publishers and authors was that if a writer had an idea for a novel, he just wrote it. The good books rose to the top and the poor ones didn't. Hamilton's book was more than a dumbed-down "how to" manual, but a serious study of how novels work. Until 1920, when William Strunk published his *Elements of Style*, Hamilton's book was the most reliable and helpful guide for both beginning and seasoned writers. Although Strunk's manual helped shape twentieth-century written English, Hamilton's guidebook influenced a whole generation of young writers, including Grey, Eugene O'Neill, Lionel Trilling, F. Scott Fitzgerald, and Ernest Hemingway.

Clayton Hamilton was a notable scholar as a young man at Columbia University, where he earned his master's degree in 1901 at the age of nineteen. He published his groundbreaking work seven years later. Above all, Hamilton related the principles and methods of fiction in a clear, lucid style. When Grey read it and considered some of its concepts, he turned quickly to writing his first Western novel, *The Heritage of the Desert* (originally titled *Mescal*). By following Hamilton's directions, Grey avoided the pitfalls and false ideas prevalent in much cheap fiction. Hamilton presented no formulas for the novel, only the essential ideas that made weak novels good and good novels better.

Grey carried around Hamilton's book throughout the autumn of 1908 and the spring of 1909, hoping for a chance to overcome *The Last of the Plainsmen*'s failure to attract a major publisher.

From the outset, Grey underlined certain words and phrases he thought important. "Every novelist of genuine importance," noted Hamilton, "seeks not only to divert but also to instruct—to instruct not abstractly, like the essayist, but concretely, by presenting to the reader characters and actions which are true." Hamilton went on to say: "the distinction between realism and romance is fundamental and deep seated; for every man, whether consciously or not, is either a romantic or realist in the dominant habit of his thought."[2] For Grey, who worried that being too much of a romantic writer would jeopardize his chances among his readers, Hamilton's words could not have come at a better time. Hamilton gave Zane Grey the permission to be a writer of Western romances.

The term "romance novel" had a far different meaning in 1910 than it does today. It was not simply a love story. It had a much broader definition to include stories of mystery and exotic places, of adventure and swashbuckling heroes. The romantic novel blossomed in the early nineteen century with the works of Jane Austen (*Pride and Prejudice*) and Charlotte Brontë (*Jane Eyre*). At the center of many of these works is the tale of lovers often impeded by insurmountable obstacles and a scornful society. The romance is generally marked by optimism and a belief that the heroine can rise above adversity. By the end of the nineteenth century, the romance novel had taken several directions, including the realms of science fiction, mystery, and detective fiction. The more serious realist writers generally derided the school of romanticism as a worn-out souvenir of the nineteenth century, preferring instead to see the world honestly and objectively. Although the romance novel has been tagged as escapist fare, it has also produced some of the great writers in fiction, such as Austen, the Brontë sisters, Robert Louis Stevenson, Arthur Conan Doyle, Edgar Allan Poe, H. G. Wells, and Herman Melville.

But Grey faced the headwinds of the publishing industry. Realism and romance in fiction had always seesawed with public taste, and in the pre–World War I age it seemed the former was dominant. The tradition of romanticist writing that stretched from Cooper to Hawthorne and Melville was being eclipsed by a group of writers intent on portraying the grim, sordid realities of American life. In 1895, Mark Twain wrote a scathing indictment of romanticist literature by attacking Fenimore Cooper and his *Leatherstocking Tales*. Twain, unfairly it can be said, claimed Cooper's work "has no invention; it has no order, sequence, system . . . its characters are confusedly drawn and by their acts and words they prove that they are not the sort of people the author claims that they are."[3] Twain's barbed assessment of Cooper's faults helped the realism movement in fiction achieve great popularity by the end of the century. The author of *The Adventures of Huckleberry Finn* remarked that romanticist fiction was "a literary dead letter after the Civil War."[4] Twain thought of American literature as linear: Cooper, Hawthorne, Melville, and the

Transcendentalists helmed the romanticist phase, which was followed by the naturalists and realists who would put to rest all this nonsense of buckskinned frontiersmen and gun-slinging cowboys tramping through forests and lassoing runaway steers. But as it turned out, literature was not linear but cyclical. Twain, and many other writers, could not envision a new phase of romanticism that produced the Western as a major genre. Energized by the advent of the motion picture industry, by the robust circulation of magazines and soft cover novels, and by the rise of Grubstreet hacks turned novelists, the Western would emerge as one of the most dominant forces in American culture for the next sixty years.

* * *

"The author of fiction who aspires to write fiction should cultivate the faculty of caring about all things that come to pass; he should train himself rigorously never to be bored; he should look upon all life that swims into his ken with curious and sympathetic eyes, remembering that sympathy is a deeper faculty than curiosity; and because of the profound joy of his interest in life, he should endeavor humbly to earn that heritage of interest by developing a thorough understanding of its source."[5] This quote from Hamilton's book remained Grey's guiding credo.

Armed with *Materials and Methods of Fiction*, Grey returned to Arizona in the spring of 1909, only to learn that Jim Emmett was in the process of moving on to Annabella, in central Utah. The LDS Church had sold its interests in Lee's Ferry to the Grand Canyon Cattle Company, thus ending the bitter dispute between Emmett and the riders of the Bar Z. Grey had difficulty letting Emmett go, for the Mormon patriarch typified all that was "rugged, splendid, and enduring."[6]

The battle between desert settlers and marauding cattle rustlers would live on, however, in Grey's *The Heritage of the Desert*, a fast-paced Western and Grey's entry into populist Western fiction. It is a quest story on two levels, as the protagonist John Hare travels to Utah in search of relief for tuberculosis and of some measure of spiritual certainty. Zane tempered his critical views of Mormon polygamy by concentrating on the nurturing aspects of Mormon culture, as mirrored in the life of August Naab, aka Jim Emmett and his family.

Mark Twain (above) was one of Harper and Brothers' stellar writers of the period. His and Zane Grey's writings intersected in a most ironic way.

In truth, Grey respected the Mormon faith. But the author, like many Americans, was alarmed by the sensationalized accounts of polygamy that had percolated through culture from the 1850s onward. Despite the fact that polygamy, or plural marriage, was outlawed by the Woodruff Manifesto of 1890, it remained a practice in certain Mormon settlements along the Utah and Arizona territorial border. Salacious reports of Mormon harems and abducted women living under the roof of oversexed men shaped Grey's view before and during his stays in Utah and Arizona. He thought that Mormon women overall were mistreated and oppressed by their husbands. Although he kept these feelings at bay through the writing of *Heritage*, they would resurface and form the sinister atmosphere of *Riders of the Purple Sage*.

He finished all five-hundred-plus handwritten pages of *The Heritage of the Desert* in autumn 1909 and turned the manuscript over to Dolly to proofread. After she thoroughly went through it, she typed two copies and then read it aloud to Zane, pausing at passages she liked and penciling out parts that troubled her. When they were convinced the manuscript was in top shape, Grey made an appointment with Ripley Hitchcock to present it to Harper for publication.

* * *

In his midlevel management position, Hitchcock considered himself the gatekeeper to the literary department and by extension the defender of the treasured legacy of Harper and Brothers. It was a legacy that stretched back to the early days of the republic, when publishers were rare and authors were rarer.

In 1817, John Harper and his brother James, both in their early twenties, opened a printing shop on the corner of Front and Dover Streets in New York. As their business grew, they were joined by their brothers Wesley and Fletcher, and together these four formed the publishing house of Harper and Brothers.

By the 1840s, the brothers were overseeing one of the largest printing facilities in the city. Before there were copyright laws involving British and American companies, book titles were commonly printed in England first, then shipped across the Atlantic to publishers in the United States.

As they became more possessive of their authors, publishers took a more independent stance. Harper reprinted several well-known British titles, including Charlotte Brontë's *Jane Eyre*, Emily Brontë's *Wuthering Heights*, William Thackeray's *Vanity Fair*, and Charles Dickens's *American Notes* and *Martin Chuzzlewit*.

America's fascination with the sea produced two writers, one of exceptional talent, Richard Henry Dana, and another of genius, Herman Melville. Dana's *Two Years Before the Mast* (1840) recorded his voyage of the brig *Pilgrim* from Boston to California. The book helped launch Dana's career as a lawyer and an advocate for seamen's rights. One of his avid readers happened to be a young Melville, who asserted in his book *White Jacket* that "his chapters on describing Cape Horn must have been written with an icicle." But Dana's title frequently confused readers unfamiliar with nautical language. The term "before the mast" indicated the quarters of sailors that were in the forecastle, located in front of the mast.[7]

Melville's parade of books for Harper included *Typee, Omoo, Mardi, Redburn,* and *White Jacket.* His novel *Moby-Dick* was first published in London by Richard Bentley. Harper had refused to pay Melville an advance because of his indebtedness to the firm. In October 1851, Bentley published the English edition, simply titled *The Whale*, limiting the first run to five hundred copies. The following month Harper published the American edition with an initial print run of nearly three thousand copies. Sales in the following months and years remained sluggish. Harper lost three hundred copies in its warehouse when it burned in 1853. *Moby-Dick* was never a blockbuster novel, selling only 3,200 copies in Melville's lifetime. Although Harper's editors always liked the book, its impact on American literature was not acknowledged until 1917, when Carl van Doren rescued it from oblivion in his critical work *The American Novel.* A few years later the British writer D. H. Lawrence lauded the novel as America's true classic and called its author "the greatest seer and poet of the sea."[8]

With much of its warehouse and editorial offices destroyed by fire, Harper and Brothers rebuilt its publishing empire, and in summer 1855 opened its new palatial facility overlooking Franklin Square. For the next fifty years, the firm continued its surge to dominance in the publishing business. As with Zane Grey, it was not always on target with its editorial decisions. In 1847, Harper agreed to publish Henry Thoreau's *A Week on the Concord and Merrimack Rivers* if the author would underwrite the printing costs. Thoreau refused and sought other publishers. In 1849, becoming frustrated, the author returned to Harper and reluctantly signed a contract. Five years later, Thoreau opted to publish *Walden* with Boston's Ticknor and Fields, leaving the Harper firm out of the book's eventual commercial success.

Harper and its main competitors—G. P. Putman and Macmillan, and later Henry Holt, Scribner's, Doubleday, and Appleton—always sought to court and retain their premier authors.

When important authors such as Dickens and Thackeray voyaged across the ocean, one of the Harper brothers met them at the dock and whisked them to a hotel near the firm. After cordial business discussions, they and other Harper authors dined at Delmonico's, where the clouds of cigar smoke were as thick as the platitudes.

After the Civil War, as Harper added its *Harper's Weekly* magazine to the production lists, illustrators rose in prominence. Winslow Homer, Howard Pyle, and Frederic Remington revealed a postbellum America through their pen-and-ink depictions. Before periodicals used photography to depict domestic and international events, Remington and Pyle used their exceptional drawing talents to make their world come alive.

By 1880, Harper and Brothers, in both prestige and commercial success, ruled the publishing empire of New York City. "My publisher is Harper's; what about yours?" became a flashy introduction between known and unknown authors. In 1885, the year *The Adventures of Huckleberry Finn* was published, Mark Twain advised William Dean Howells, presently without a publisher, to go "with Harper's. I have noticed that good men in their employ go there to stay." Twain was a regular at the House of Harper, showing up in his trademark immaculate suit, with wizard-white hair and his cigar dangling from his fingers.[9]

Harper's façade on Pearl Street and Franklin Square had begun to show signs of wear, as the city matured and spread its commercial might in all directions. Running in front of Harper, the elevated train rumbled by so loudly that it shook the panes of glass on the third floor. Traffic on the nearby Brooklyn Bridge was ceaseless. The Lower East Side had become a warren of shacks, brownstones, and tenements filled by constant shiploads of immigrants and disgruntled Southerners.

In 1890, after a brief stint at the *New York Sun*, Richard Harding Davis took over the helm of *Harper's Weekly*, a plum assignment that mirrored his ambition. Although he gained fame as a reporter in the Spanish-American War eight years later, he achieved experience in other aspects of writing as editor of the *Weekly*. Harper's flagship magazines, *Harper's Weekly*, *Harper's Monthly*, and *Harper's Bazaar*, boosted the publishing firm's already premier reputation. Davis attracted a flock of talented writers, including Bret Harte, Mark Twain, Hamlin Garland, and Owen Wister.

In contrast to Harte's colorful West, Wister offered a more sober, carefully studied territory packed with mannered cowboys, educated women, and loudmouth villains. His Western towns, such as Medicine Bow, Wyoming, are representative of many of the instant towns of the West. The houses "seemed to have been strewn there by the wind and to be waiting till the wind should come again and blow them away," Wister wrote in *The Virginian*. "Yet serene above their foulness swam a pure and quiet light, such as the East never sees; they might be bathing in the air of creation's first morning."[10] Across Wyoming and Nebraska were thousands of ramshackle towns, with shotgun shanties leaning against weary saloons and with rutted main streets becoming lakes of mud and ooze.

Owen Wister was an Ivy League original—a Harvard grad—who waxed the ends of his mustache and wore tall leather boots. He wore a cowboy hat and a suit tailored on Fifth Avenue. He arrived in New York believing he was a planet among shooting stars and possessing the qualities Grey lacked, most notably breeding and self-confidence. Wister's life appeared well integrated between writing, traveling, and conversing with genteel companions in nicely furnished saloons.

Davis was impressed with Owen when they met in the offices of *Harper's Weekly* in 1891. Wister carried a well-written short story he had penned, "Hank's Woman." Davis liked its veracity and realistic treatment of the West. Wister's snapshots of the West and his nuanced characters combined to make a readable short work.

Published in 1892, "Hank's Woman" set the precedent for the popular Western, which culminated in Wister's novel *The Virginian* of 1902.

Author of *The Virginian* and other Western works, Owen Wister was a writer with exceptional talent and perceptive ability.

The story opens with some brilliant imagery, followed by an even more brilliant simile: "Westward, the Tetons lifted their peaks pale and keen as steel through the high, radiant air. Deep down between the blue gashes of their canyons the sun sank long shafts of light, and the glazed laps of their snow-fields shone separate and white upon their lofty vastness, like handkerchiefs laid out to dry."[11] Wister's descriptions often teeter on the brink of sensory overload but rarely collapse.

Throughout his career, Wister credited the West for saving his sanity and physical health. In 1885, close to a nervous breakdown, he journeyed west from Philadelphia and stayed at a ranch near Glenrock, Wyoming. The brief visit restored his health and confirmed that the West was pure goodness for the soul. His work never penetrated the land beyond the Rockies, but the rarefied air of Wyoming was substantial enough on which to base most of his writing.

Wister was a better stylist and had a more imaginative authorial voice than Zane Grey. Grey devoured *The Virginian* and wanted to follow in the footsteps of Wister. Whether Grey would have developed and mastered the popular Western without Wister's lead is a matter of debate.

Wister was a mythmaker and reporter of singular skill. His ability to distill the essence of a scene was exceptional in Western writing at the end of the nineteenth century, but so too were his distracting habits of mixing politics and racial stereotypes. He disliked the populist message of the times, preferring to believe that the cowpuncher was heir to the Anglo-Saxon knighthood tradition. The West was a vastly different country than New York or Boston, claimed Wister, a message Grey revitalized in *Riders of the Purple Sage*.

Wister stayed with Harper and Brothers until 1900, when the firm, quite suddenly, declared bankruptcy. Under a reorganization plan, it returned to business and named Colonel George Harvey as its president. The company started generating revenue again, and many authors returned to the fold, including Mark Twain and William Dean Howells. Frederick Duneka was brought in as general manager and began a long tenure grooming and retaining authors. He tried his best to re-sign Wister, but the sudden rupture of Harper's business scared Owen into seeking a more lucrative contract with Macmillan. Thus, *The Virginian* and Owen

Wister were viewed by Harper's editors as the ones that got away. *The Virginian* headed the best-seller lists in 1902 and settled in the number five spot the following year. Wister ended up writing a stage adaptation of the novel in 1903, which ran for ten years. Since then, no one has particularly objected to the idea that he was the father of the popular Western.

Sometimes called the "Victor Hugo of the North," Rex Beach returned from the Klondike in 1904, lacking both gold and a reputation as a novelist. But Frederick Duneka, unwilling to make the same mistake as Harper did with Owen Wister, signed Beach to a one-book contract for *The Spoilers*. The book soared in popularity and was the number eight best seller in 1906. He repeated his good fortune in 1908 with *The Barrier*, and again in 1909 with *The Silver Horde*. By then Ripley Hitchcock was his editor, although Duneka had the final word on contracts. Harper remained on the lookout for fabulists like Beach who could write two-fisted action novels that sold well.

And so it was with some trepidation that Hitchcock received a note from Grey concerning another book from the author. Hitchcock had the good name of Harper and Brothers to uphold. He also was not about to lose another Stephen Crane or Owen Wister.

CHAPTER SIX

A Horseman Riding By

On March 2, 1910, Zane Grey stepped from the train and steered toward Ripley Hitchcock's office.

In 1910, New York City had a population of four million souls, and they all seemed to gather on the sidewalks and streets, in carriages and motorcars, kiosks and street corners, speaking in English, Russian, and Polish, the smoke from their pipes and cigars drifting over their din and up into the smirched white or pale blue skies. Once inside Hitchcock's office, Grey quickly handed him the manuscript of *The Heritage of the Desert*. Before the editor could mutter a word, Grey blurted out, "Mr. Hitchcock, I know you are convinced that I cannot write fiction, but this is the type of book I have always wanted to write. I have worked harder on it than any other book I have done. I believe it is a good book. I will never bother you again. I only ask as a personal favor that you read this manuscript yourself."[1]

Because it was so difficult to get the words out, Grey had rehearsed his plea while on the train ride from Lackawaxen. After returning to Pennsylvania, he waited for Hitchcock's reply. And he waited. These were the worst of times for a writer. He had spent most of his and Dolly's money on the trips west, and he had banked everything on this book. All the negative voices came back to him, telling him how foolish it was to have even picked up a pencil in the first place and then have the nerve to put his family through all the disappointment.

Moreover, he was growing old. He was thirty-eight, with forty staring him in the face. Silver streaked his hair; his face was leathery and a burnished red from the Arizona sun, and crow's feet appeared by his eyes. He

The crowded streets of Lower Manhattan in 1910

was aging, but to his credit he did not feel old. Rather, he always maintained a youthful body and spirit. No matter what he ate—eggs, beef, pork, bread, beans, or hardtack, he rarely gained weight. His constant movement and activity helped his mood swings and activated a body meant for fishing, hiking, horseback riding, and roping lions in Arizona. He realized he was a latecomer to the writing game. But he was steadfast and triumphant in spirit and somehow believed that he could overcome the many rejections and barriers he faced. Writing was a lot of dirty work—starting, stopping, rewriting, correcting, and polishing—but all the drudgery was lost in the reward of a day's good work. He had become patient with editors. Whether it would last was another matter.

Within a few days he stood in Hitchcock's office, braced for another disappointment. Instead, Hitchcock smiled and shook his hand. "Grey, I've read *The Heritage of the Desert*. You've done it. You've made me eat my words. It's a fine novel, and here's proof of it." Hitchcock handed the author Harper's blue contract.[2]

Grey's legs started shaking, then his hand. He grabbed the pen in his fingers and scrawled his name. It was barely legible. His body was still trembling as he left the editor's office and shambled down the stairs. Later, after he had collected his senses, he wrote about Hitchcock in his diary: "How strange that he, who has tortured me, should be the one to encourage me! He expressed a specific and personal interest in me and my future, and wants to form a kind of partnership with me, in which I am to profit by his knowledge and suggestions ... He is very smooth, perhaps deep, and I won't go so far as to say hypocritical. But I'll meet him halfway, and be earnest and sincere in my work to do what he wants. Then we'll see. Whatever he means I am indebted to him. I am grateful. For now the real work begins."[3]

The Heritage of the Desert was published in September 1910 and sales quickly passed the thirty thousand mark. Editors at Harper were elated, particularly Ripley Hitchcock and his boss, Frederick Duneka.

Grey's first Western novel was the pacesetter for most of his ensuing work. He had added voltage to the popular genre, virtually energizing it at a time when it was ripe for commercialization. It was Cooper, Harte,

Buntline, and Wister repackaged for the twentieth century. Grey ended up celebrating his accomplishment, but it was only the beginning.

There were several reasons Grey's first Western and his subsequent hit, *Riders of the Purple Sage,* were so phenomenally successful. The first reason was that Grey enjoyed telling tales—the first sign of a good story-teller. As Clayton Hamilton suggested in *Materials and Methods of Fiction*: "In the great storytellers, there is a sort of self-enjoyment in the exercise in the sense of narrative; and this, by sheer contagion, communicates enjoyment to the reader . . . and surely it is not frivolous to state that the most profound and serious of thoughts are communicated best when they are communicated with the greatest interest."[4] Despite all his faults as a writer, Grey loved the West, and he communicated that love through his early fiction.

The second reason is also apparent. Grey was an irreclaimable romantic. He could communicate to his readers both what he knew about the West and what he imagined it to be. According to Hamilton, the romantic "feels no obligation to make the imagined facts of his story resemble closely the details of actual life; he is anxious only that they shall represent his idea adequately and consistently." The writer of romance, said Hamilton, "need not provide evidence to support his theme. . . . The romantic says: 'These things are so, because I know they are' . . . A great romantic, therefore, must have the wisdom that convinces by its very presence and conquers credence through the reader's intuition."[5] In Grey's initial fiction, especially in *The Heritage of the Desert* and *Riders of the Purple Sage,* this lean toward romance is especially strong. Although many readers of the time may not have been well versed in the West, they believed this is the way it actually was.

Writing in the early twentieth century had changed since the days of Melville, Hawthorne, and even early Twain. Instead of long, meandering sentences and innocent disquisitions, this age demanded speed in everything. As *Life* magazine put it: "This is a get-things-done-quick age. It is a ready-to-put-on-and-wear home age, a just-add-water-and-serve age, a take it or leave it, I'm very busy age."[6] Like culture, prose had to *move*. Rather than spend time setting a scene, writers jumped right into it. The highest-paid authors of the age, who included Owen Wister, Jack

London, Richard Harding Davis, and Booth Tarkington, all felt the urge to liven the pace of their stories. After all, they had to compete with sensationalized murders, kidnappings, battle reports, and impending divorces of the rich and powerful.

Romance has been traditionally viewed as plot-driven; realistic writing is generally character-driven. To begin a story, Grey had three options: he could choose a plot and let the characters and situations develop from it; or he could select his characters and shape the narrative around them; or, a less popular alternative, he could pick a place and mold his characters and situations around it. In *The Heritage of the Desert*, he selected Jim Emmett, aka August Naab, as the base of his story. Although the novel eventually became plot-driven, it started out as a character-based novel.

The Heritage of the Desert relates the story of John Hare, a greenhorn Easterner suffering from tuberculosis who travels to the Southwest in search of a cure for his illness. Faced with imminent death, he wanders from village to village but quickly becomes disoriented in the maze of canyons and mesas. Dying of exhaustion, hunger, and thirst, he is discovered by August Naab, a Mormon cattle rancher and patriarch. The faithful Naab will not let Hare suffer, even when the Mormon is threatened by rustlers, outlaws, and Gentile ranchers.

Grey describes his desert host and healer this way: "August Naab was close to three score years; his chest was as wide as a door; his arm like the branch of an oak. He was a blacksmith, a mechanic, a carpenter, a cooper, a porter. At his forge and in his shop, everywhere were crude tools, wagons, farming implements, sets of buckskin harness, odds and ends of nameless things eloquent and pregnant proof of the fact that necessity is the mother of invention . . . he was a farmer, a cattleman, a grafter of fruit trees. . . . Best and strangest of all in this wonderful man was the instinct and heart to heal."[7]

Naab assumes care of the ailing man and raises him as his son. He instructs Hare in the ways of the desert: riding horses, firing weapons, and surviving in the blanched terrain. Considered a spy for the government by the outlaws, Hare soon becomes embroiled in a land war for control of the territory. But Hare commits the dangerous sin of wooing the half-Indian woman Mescal, who, unbeknownst to Hare, is pledged to become the second wife of August's quixotic son.

The outlaw gang raids Naab's lands and steals his cattle. But Naab, adhering to his faith, refuses to retaliate. After several minor knots in the storyline are untied—the flight of Mescal to the wilderness, the revenge of Naab's son against his father, the murder of August's son by the outlaw Holderness, and the killing of Holderness by John Hare—the reader is ready to encounter the major knot.

August Naab, the stoic, pacifist Mormon, turns into the vengeful rancher by embracing his own sense of frontier justice. Portrayed as a static character initially, he becomes a dynamic one by subduing the outlaws and achieving heroic stature in the eyes of Hare and Mescal. As a result, Hare and Mescal, now married, are included in Naab's family and become heirs to the Mormon's empire. John Hare, through education by Naab and by his defeat of the outlaws, learns the heritage of the desert, the value of love, and the bounds of faith.

The Heritage of the Desert contains one of the story arcs of romanticist fiction: the hero has a need that becomes a quest; then he is helped by a wise authority figure, who teaches him the ways of his environment. The hero matures, achieving wisdom and courage, then subdues his enemies and wins the hand of a lady—in this case an earth goddess. The story moves through several layers of rising and falling tension but generally concludes with the hero and his companions rewarded in some fashion.

One of the main features of romanticism is to realize the desirable, and so the arc proceeds from darkness to a measure of light. For the reader it is ultimately wish fulfillment, as well as an interesting journey through the hero's struggle.

If all of these details seem familiar, it is because Grey lived them. Grey based most of his plot on the ongoing battle between Jim Emmett and the Grand Canyon Cattle Company. He added the neophyte John Hare to the dirty dealings, mixed in some "sealed marriage" features to stir up some villainy to the plot, and turned the outlaws loose on Naab's land and family. But these often facile actions do not detract from Grey's story, because the author has strong enough narrative capabilities to overcome any trivial plot points.

Grey soon realized that the publication of a first novel brings with it high expectations for the next book. The performance bar is raised significantly for the writer's second offering. Still, he reflected on his good fortune. "Something really vital and wonderful has happened—," he remarked in his diary, "Harper and Brothers [sic] acceptance of my desert romance. I do not seem to realize it. I am glad, of course, but the wild joy I thought I'd feel is not manifest. A panicky feeling seems to be the strongest, a fear that I might not reach up to Mr. Hitchcock's estimate of me. He praised my work and pointed out my faults. Still I am too flowery, too self-conscious, stilted, strained. I must ease up in my terse work. More restraint. The strangeness and aloofness I feel for my characters must be remedied. I must put in the little significant touches that will make the story rise up stirring and warm with life."[8]

* * *

After the publication of *Heritage*, things in the author's life shifted dramatically. Dr. Zane Grey, former tooth puller, Grubstreet warhorse, and ex-Manhattan cliff dweller, had become something of an overnight sensation in the book world. He did not want to count his fledglings just yet, however, as he worked on the manuscript of his next novel. He planned on making it his longest work yet, well over a hundred thousand words and brimming with the simmering energy that characterized the final chapters of *The Heritage of the Desert*.

In 1910 and again the following year, Zane returned to the northern Arizona border in yet another scouting of the area. This time he toured the land near Kayenta, where he hoped to secure the talents of John Wetherill. Grey's goal was to reach the Rainbow Bridge in southern Utah. But Wetherill was not available when he reached Kayenta, which prompted him to begin his trek to Betatakin Canyon and continue on to Keet Seel, a set of ancient cliff dwellings. On this particular journey, he made it as far as Tsegi Canyon, about twenty miles southwest of Kayenta.

Tsegi Canyon contains a lush forested belt surmounted by steep cliffs. If there is a Shangri-la in the Southwest, it is here. Grey quickly noticed its possibilities for his romantic fiction. It was the perfect hiding place for fugitives and lovers escaping the malicious forces that threatened them. "I

Betatakin Canyon, part of the Navajo National Monument, is similar to the terrain of Surprise Valley in Zane's most famous novel.

JEFFREY M. FRANK @SHUTTERSTOCK.COM

climbed high upon the huge stones," Grey wrote, "and I entered the musty cliff dwellings, and called out to hear the weird and sonorous echoes. . . . I wandered through the thickets and upon the grassy spruce-shaded benches."[9] He gave it the fictional name Surprise Valley, and for several moments he paused in the shade of an old juniper, filling the canyon with shadows and sounds from his imagination.

On the same trip he sojourned in Kanab. One morning he saw a horseman riding down the edge of the main street; he was a Mormon resident dressed in dark coat and hat and sitting nobly astride his mount. He paid no attention to Grey, but rather guided his horse to a corner, turned, and was gone. The author seized the moment.

A horseman riding by. It was as simple as that. Suddenly, his mind started working out the parts of the story: how a dark-clad stranger, virtually from nowhere, appears to intervene between the forces of good and those of evil. He would embody the code of the West and bring an intuitive knowledge of law and morality to the territory. The character of Jim Lassiter arrived through the most humdrum of means.

Thus, the events in *Riders of the Purple Sage* began in Kanab and spread to Tsegi Canyon and Deception Pass in northern Arizona. Grey worked on the manuscript in both Utah and Arizona throughout the summer and fall of 1911. Grey was quite aware that his treatment of the intractable Mormon theocracy in southern Utah would create more hostilities toward the LDS Church. He had no intention of continuing the assault on the Mormon faith that had been perpetrated by a score of books since the middle of the last century. Fiction as well as nonfiction attacked the lurid aspects of Mormon forced marriage and blood atonement: John Hansen Beadle's *Life in Utah; or, The Mysteries and Crimes of Mormonism* and Cornelia Paddock's *The Fate of Madame La Tour* were but two examples.

But perhaps the most sensationalized account, and by far the most popular, was Arthur Conan Doyle's *A Study in Scarlet*, which detailed how a woman died of a broken heart after settling for a sealed marriage. Like Grey in *Riders of the Purple Sage*, Doyle needed a plot of some malice to motivate his characters to action. Doyle later retracted his statements in *A Study in Scarlet* by saying that he used "rather sensational and over-colored pictures" of Mormonism in early Utah. But the damage had been done. Conan Doyle's depictions heightened the suspicions of an entire generation.

Grey's creation of Jane Withersteen in the central role in *Riders* was one of his most successful characterizations. As a woman torn between her faith and her own instinctive sense of morality, she undergoes an intense inward journey. Despite Lassiter's scene-stealing black garb, Withersteen is the most profound character in the novel. It is little wonder that Grey based her character on Dolly Grey, his wife and most trusted friend.

Grey wrote *Riders of the Purple Sage* in pencil and, as was customary, turned it over to Dolly to proofread and type two copies. She was thrilled by its characters and storyline. Zane debated whether to serialize the story with the Frank Munsey Company or send it directly to Ripley Hitchcock at Harper and Brothers. Serialization meant quick royalties, but publication at Harper would give the novel a higher standing with critics.

Grey thought that he understood Ripley Hitchcock and that the submission of *Riders* would be a smooth process. He delivered the hefty manuscript to the senior editor, who promised a speedy reply. The author also dropped off a copy to Bob Davis, the editor of *Munsey's*, hoping that the publisher would jump at a serialization of the book.

But once again, the rains came down. Davis explained to Grey that his readership would be deeply offended by the treatment of Mormons in the novel. Even non-Mormons, Davis feared, would be distressed by Grey's depictions. The editors of *Popular* magazine also shied away from publishing it.

A short time later, Hitchcock echoed Davis's concerns and reported that Harper could not publish the manuscript. In addition to the distasteful treatment of Mormons, Harper's editors also found it a bit "bludgy"— meaning an easy read. Grey did not take the news well.

But Hitchcock's report was not entirely dismal. He told Zane that he would forward the manuscript upstairs to Frederick Duneka, who would make the final decision on the novel. And with this news, Grey retreated to Pennsylvania to await *Riders'* fate.

*　*　*

The Harper and Brothers power structure was known throughout New York publishing circles. At the top of the pecking order was the acid-tongued president, George Harvey, known simply as the Colonel. Next in line was Frederick Duneka, who supervised the day-to-day operations as well as scouting and retaining the best authors. Harvey was a political progressive who later served as US ambassador to Great Britain under President Woodrow Wilson. Duneka was a devout Roman Catholic and a charmer without a hint of arrogance.

When Duneka received *Riders of the Purple Sage* from Hitchcock, he was deeply involved in editing another project. After Mark Twain's death in April 1910, his literary executor, Albert Bigelow Paine, partnered with Duneka to edit and issue Twain's previously unpublished manuscript "A Chronicle of Young Satan." It was published by Harper in 1916 under the title *The Mysterious Stranger*. Penned intermittently between 1897 and 1908, Twain's work was in reality three stories cobbled together to make one bitter, uneven novel.

By possessing all of Twain's unfinished work, Paine was able to direct most of the editorial decisions. But Duneka had the final word about what Harper was willing to publish. Duneka worked on and off for three years on Twain's novel, laboring over the anti-Catholic passages and saving the more scurrilous ones for his scalpel. Violating many of his principles, *The Mysterious Stranger* irritated Duneka endlessly. Twain's condemnation of religion, his scenes of hangings, burnings at the stake, and gruesome deaths challenged Duneka's Jesuit upbringing. Moreover, Twain's nihilism in the person of Satan seemed to deal a crushing blow to Duneka's and the nation's peaceful certainties. "There is no God," Satan declares, "no heaven, no hell. It is all a dream—a grotesque and foolish dream. Nothing exists but you. And you are but a thought, a homeless thought, wandering forlorn among the empty eternities." In a novel filled with darkness and arctic chill, Duneka struggled to render it presentable to Harper's readers.

Thus, when he received Zane Grey's second Western novel, he was initially surprised by yet another author exposing religious fanaticism. Grey's novel was far tamer, but Duneka still worried about a backlash from the readership. He considered it a better novel than *Heritage of the Desert*, but he was tempted to strike out some of the more salacious passages involving the Mormon faith. Although there were no references to the evils of Catholicism in Grey's book, Duneka bristled at the inflammatory references to sealed marriages, blood atonement, and women possessed by religious madmen. Religion, Duneka believed, was supposed to promote the better angels of our natures. It was not meant to demean, punish, torment, isolate, or threaten the very souls it was intended to comfort.

Despite his misgivings, Duneka wanted to publish *Riders of the Purple Sage*. He liked Grey's vivid descriptions of the desert landscape integrated with the action scenes. Grey gave the reader a true sense of the vastness and mystery of the desert, as well as a glimpse of the lonely, cavalier horsemen of the Old West.

Duneka delayed his final decision a few days, during which time his wife read Grey's manuscript. When she responded favorably to it, Duneka asked Grey in to sign a contract. While Harper was considering his novel, Grey had queried his friend Eltinge Warner of *Field and Stream* about serializing *Riders of the Purple Sage* in the magazine.

And so it was that *Riders* first ran in installments, beginning in January 1912, before Harper and Brothers published it later that year.

CHAPTER SEVEN

Inside *Riders*

A GOOD NOVEL DISCLOSES THE MINDSET OF THE TIME; A GREAT NOVEL reveals the consciousness of the age. This is not to say that *Riders of the Purple Sage* belongs in the same company as, say, Hawthorne's *Scarlet Letter* or Crane's *Red Badge of Courage*. But along with Owen Wister's *The Virginian*, it is one of the best popular Westerns from that era or from any era. It contains the features that reflect the consciousness of those years before and after the Great War in Europe, when humanity needed some escape route from the horrific realties of mechanized warfare. The country sought an identity of its own, and the mythic American West was open for business.

The treatment of Mormons in the novel hung over Harper's management like a dense fog during the editorial process. It was clear to Duneka that Grey was not indicting all Mormons, just those with fanatical beliefs in a particular community at a particular time. This knowledge was important to Duneka because he wanted to avoid any insinuation that this novel was an attack on the LDS Church. Any reasonable person, concluded Duneka, would be able to distinguish the beliefs of one individual from those of the religion as a whole. As a precaution, however, he kept his eyes on *Field and Stream*'s January issue for any adverse reaction to Grey's novel. He heard no reports of any outraged Mormons or non-Mormons. The book passed the "canary in the coal mine" test through several key installments in the magazine. Assured now, Duneka and Hitchcock were ready to move to the next editorial step.

Grey rushed through his manuscripts, often at blinding speed. One of the first features to suffer was his diction. Duneka and the copy editor were able to correct some of the more significant blunders in Grey's wording, and then ensure that the tone was consistent throughout.

Riders did not crack the top ten best-seller lists for 1912 or the following year, but it did add fuel to Grey's reputation. Everyone—publishers, editors, agents—were on the lookout for the next Zane Grey. Grey could, as they say, write his own ticket to anywhere, but most people knew he only wanted to travel in one direction.

Riders of the Purple Sage is a complex novel, full of encounters, revelations, searches, and unmaskings. Despite its stylistic flaws, melodramatic dialogue, cloying flirtations, and improbable trysts, it remains one of the best of Zane Grey's creations.

* * *

The novel opens in Utah Territory in the year 1871, when the railroad and several gold strikes have brought waves of Gentiles into the valleys that Mormons previously settled. Friction and resentment have developed between the two groups; outlaw bands have raided Mormon communities and harassed anyone in their path. It is generally a lawless territory ruled by intractable Mormons and rowdy outlaws.

Riders features the stunning terrain around Kanab, Utah, a blend of winding canyons; bold, crenellated mesas; and the dun-colored, high desert sands spangled with purple sage. The novel sweeps into northern Arizona to include Tsegi Canyon and Deception Pass, but Grey abbreviates the distance from Kanab to these points for the sake of the narrative. At times, Grey has to prevent this landscape from being the hero of his novel—so great is his connection to this region. As Hamilton pointed out: "The aim of description—which is to suggest the look of things in a characteristic moment—is an aim necessarily static. But life—which the artist proposes to represent—is not static but dynamic. The aim of description is pictorial: but life does hold its pictures; it melts and merges them into one another with headlong hurrying progression. A novelist, who devotes two successive pages to the landscape or person, necessarily makes his story stand still while he is doing it, and thereby belies an obvious law of life."[1]

Twenty-eight-year-old Jane Withersteen has inherited a ranch from her father called Cottonwoods. She has been "promised" to polygamist

With illustrations by Douglas Duer, the first edition of *Riders of the Purple Sage* hit the bookshelves in 1912, and it has since remained Grey's crowning achievement in Western storytelling.

Elder Tull in marriage but has successfully resisted his advances—till now. She insists she will marry for love, rather than obey the dictates of the church.

One of her hired cowhands is Bern Venters, a man from Illinois who has been in the territory for eight years and has run afoul of the Mormons residing nearby. Elder Tull, who views Venters as a Gentile interloper, shows up one day at Jane's ranch along with his riders to punish Venters, whom they suspect of trying to court Jane. The Mormons have chosen whipping—a form of blood atonement—to subdue Venters. Tull and his henchmen seize Venters and prepare to unleash their punishment.

Into this fierce skirmish rides the most feared man in the territory, the black-clad, gun-slinging, Mormon-hater Jim Lassiter. A grim stare-down ensues between Lassiter and Tull and his band, as the former comes to the aid of Venters and Jane. Lassiter listens to Jane and Venters as they explain the injustice of the situation.

Tull snarls at Lassiter: "Here, stranger, this is none of your mix. Don't try any interference. . . . Water your horse and be on your way."

Tull reminds the mounted stranger that he is transgressing Mormon law.

"To hell with Mormon law," barks Lassiter.[2]

Tull and his men withdraw, saving their vengeance for another day.

This initial standoff in chapter 1 creates the tension throughout the novel. Through it the personalities and desires of the central characters are partially revealed. Grey purposely used a "quick entry" into the action and allowed for the greater shaping of the characters to occur chapter by chapter. To achieve the necessary connection with his fictitious characters, he created people who are worth knowing. "Since he aims to make his readers intimate with his characters," noted Clayton Hamilton, "an author must first of all be careful that his characters are worth knowing intimately."[3] Any breakdown in this connection will force a novel to plummet quickly.

Riders of the Purple Sage contains several personalities worthy of our trust, including the central characters of Jim Lassiter and Jane Withersteen. Raised in the Mormon faith, Jane has always obeyed the church and its teachings. Lassiter is a former Texas Ranger who has searched

Chapter 1

Lassiter.

A sharp clip-clop of iron-shod hoofs deadened and died away, and clouds of yellow-dust drifted from under the cottonwoods out over the sage.

Jane Withersteen gazed down the wide purple slope with dreamy and troubled eyes. A rider had just left her and it was his message that held her thoughtful and almost sad, awaiting the churchmen who were coming to resent and attack her right to befriend a Gentile.

She wondered if the unrest and strife that had lately come to the little village of Cottonwoods was to involve her. And then she sighed, remembering that her father had founded this remotest border settlement of Southern Utah, and that he had left it to her. She owned all the ground and many of the cottages. Withersteen House was here and the great ranch with its thousands of cattle, and the swiftest horses of the sage. To her belonged Amber Spring, the water which gave verdure and beauty to the village and made living possible on that wild purple upland waste. She could not escape being involved by whatever befell Cottonwoods.

That year, 1871, had marked a change which had been gradually coming in the lives

This is Zane Grey's original handwritten first page of chapter 1 of *Riders of the Purple Sage*.

from town to town, looking for the Mormon who persuaded Lassiter's sister Milly to leave her husband and settle in Utah. Lassiter's quest is more of a mission than a search. He resents proselytizing Mormons who coerce unsuspecting women to become part of their "harem."

Jane, like other notable heroines in American fiction, including Hester Prynne in *The Scarlet Letter* and Daisy Miller, the eponymous character of a Henry James novel, is the proud and pivotal figure in Grey's story. Raised as a Mormon, Jane breaks through the conventions and restrictions of her time and remains spirited and defiant. Brave and flirtatious, Jane possesses a troubled heart. She longs for the day Mormons and

Page two of Zane's draft of the novel
COURTESY OF THE OHIO HISTORY CONNECTION
OM1464_153422_002

Gentiles will live peacefully, when Mormon women can overcome their subservient roles and roving men will no longer carry guns to settle their disputes. Lassiter both pities and admires Jane. He calls Mormon women "the best and noblest, the most long-suffering, and the blindest, unhappiest women on earth."[4] One of her Mormon friends tells her: "You must choose between the love of man and the love of God." Her friend also instructs her to "marry Tull. It's your duty as a Mormon. . . . You'll feel no rapture as his wife—but think of Heaven! Mormon women don't marry for what they expect on earth." Torn between the riches of earth and heaven, her will and her faith, she seeks comfort with Lassiter. But Jane is not blind to injustice, nor will she refuse to aid Gentiles such as Venters and Lassiter. The theme of blindness pervades this novel: Lassiter's blind revenge; his horse's physical blindness caused by Mormons; Tull's violent intolerance of Gentiles; and the blind canyons that hide men, outlaws, and their folly.

Jane may be proud, but she is not blind to hatred. "Her forefathers had been Vikings," writes Grey, "savage chieftains who bore no cross and brooked no hindrance to their will. Her father had inherited that temper; and at times like an antelope fleeing before fire on the slope, his people fled from his red rages. . . . She shrank from black depths hitherto unsuspected. The one thing in man or woman that she scorned above all scorn, and which she could not forgive, was hate. Hate headed a flaming pathway straight to hell. . . . And the man who had dragged her peaceful and loving spirit to this degradation was a minister of God's word, an Elder of the church, the counselor of her beloved Bishop."[5]

Shunned by her church community for openly defying its covenants on plural marriage, Jane turns to the outcasts in her midst, Lassiter and Venters. In their company she becomes aware of her own beauty and attractiveness. Looking in the mirror, she tries to sort out her feelings: "Her relatives and friends, and later a horde of Mormon and Gentile suitors, had fanned the flame of natural vanity in her. So that at twenty-eight she scarcely thought at all of her wonderful influence for good in the little community where her father had left her practically its beneficent landlord, but cared most for the dream and the assurance and the allurement of her beauty. . . . she wondered if she were to seem fair in the eyes of this

Lassiter, this man whose name had crossed the long, wild brakes of stone and plains of sage, this gentle-voiced, sad-faced man who was a hater and a killer of Mormons."[6]

As the noble owner of Cottonwoods, Jane feels that she is in a position to shape the attitudes of the surrounding communities. She takes Venters's guns and then aims for Lassiter's. Jane returns their weapons only when they ride out to fight the outlaw gang headed by Oldring and his Masked Rider. Tull and the outlaws are in league to suppress any Gentile interference in their scheme to dominate the territory.

Enter Jim Lassiter, seemingly a man from nowhere heading nowhere, the prototype of the stern, laconic horseman with a sense of justice. "There are only two plots," critic John Gardner once noted: "A man goes on a journey; a stranger comes to town." If this true, then Lassiter covers both storylines as he arrives at Jane's estate.

There is always an aura of mystery about men from nowhere, although Grey establishes that he is a former Texas Ranger, to give him some background in law and order. Lassiter's lineage stretches back to Galahad and Percival, Gawain and Deerslayer, eventually widening to include real-life lawmen like Wyatt Earp and John Hughes. Although not as legendary as Earp, Texas Ranger Hughes roamed from Texas to the New Mexico Badlands, pursuing bandits and horse rustlers, chalking up one of the best track records for arrests in the Old West. In addition to inspiring the character of Lassiter in *Riders*, Hughes also appears in Grey's later work *The Lone Star Ranger*.

Whether Elder Tull, Oldring, or Bishop Dyer accept the idea or not, Jim Lassiter is the de facto lawman in Cottonwoods. His very presence insists on this: the black garb, the restless gun at his hip, "and the intensity of his gaze . . . a piercing wistfulness of keen gray sight, as if the man was forever looking for that which he never found."[7]

One clever way Grey uses to delineate Lassiter's personality is to have the other characters announce his arrival, a device that removes the author from the omniscient voice and makes the narrative more artful. In the opening sequence, Lassiter approaches from a ridge near Cottonwoods; Jane, Venters, and Tull and his riders glance up at the dark figure against the sun.

One of Tull's band points to the horseman and exclaims: "Look!"

"A rider," says another.

"Do you know him? Does anyone know him?" snarls Tull.

His riders shake their heads.

"He's come from far," a rider concludes.

Another adds, "That's a fine hoss."

"A strange rider. Huh! He wears black leather!"

As Lassiter comes nearer, one of Tull's men whispers, "Look! He packs two black-butted guns—low down—they're hard to see—black akin them black chaps."

"A gun-man! Fellers, careful now about movin' your hands."[8]

From these remarks we learn a good deal, without the author having to say a word.

Lassiter, Venters, and the other riders possess four characteristics common to men and women of the high desert sage: (1) the need for freedom that is absolute and unyielding; (2) the presence of loneliness, which is often carved into their faces; (3) the need for connection to some living thing; and (4) the awareness of death, which is always near. The legendary Arthurian hero remains alive in the horsemen of the West, bringing a clear sense of morality to a virtually lawless world.

Mormon law, therefore, confuses Lassiter and Venters. Polygamy in their eyes is slavery, pure and simple.

If Lassiter is a knight without armor, Bern Venters has no need of such noble trappings. Venters is a salt-of-the-earth cowboy, a man who finds pleasure in sleeping out on the sage.

As one of her riders, he has a soft crush on Jane. In return, Jane shelters him from the wrath of Tull. She warms to Venters's protective nature, but she gives her heart to Lassiter.

Once she has identified her feelings for Lassiter, she aims to ensure he does not kill any Mormons in the community. She tries to take his guns. Jane envisions that another way to keep Lassiter safe is to have him sojourn at her ranch a while longer. In either case, the oozing of Jane's charm begins to erode Lassiter's granite surface, and soon the Texan is ensnared. Silencing Lassiter's guns becomes her mission, for she views that success as a road to her romance with him. But in a larger sense, Jane yearns for peace and harmony in southwestern Utah Territory, and if she can use her talents to engender that she will go to great lengths to do so.

Elder Tull and his superior, Bishop Dyer, are Lassiter's villains-in-waiting. Together and in league with Oldring they threaten, coerce, and intimidate Jane into becoming a passive Mormon woman. When Tull is thwarted in his quest to marry Jane, he turns his sights on the Withersteen empire and its cattle herds. Eventually, Jane's wranglers, ranch hands, and female help, fearful of attack, flee Cottonwoods. The herds on several ranges begin to dwindle. Tull's pressure appears insistent and all-consuming.

Evil characters must be properly motivated. Tull is a convincing character because his motivations are true to his convictions. He believes that Jane is his property. Only a person motivated by this sense of self-righteous anger can be genuine. We can see him trying to tear Venters from Jane's grasp: his gray hair poking like straw from under his black hat, the menacing lips turned downward in a sneer, and the taut frame ready to unleash its wrath.

It seems that the dark legacy of John D. Lee affected Grey deeply.

* * *

Most linear art forms, such as fiction and music, have points of tension and release. The novel in particular has less significant points, the minor knots, along the way to the culminating point of tension, the major knot. In *Riders of the Purple Sage* the major knot answers the questions: Who coerced Lassiter's sister into leaving Texas and settling in Utah as a Mormon wife? And what became of sister Milly and her child as a result of her forced marriage to an unknown Mormon? Lassiter's search involves several minor knots in the story that need untying.

Grey, as the writer and artist, weaves together the strands of his plot so that they come together in a common culmination. During this process, Grey creates one or a series of complications and their resolutions that stand at the height of each series. The point of greatest complication of the whole novel—the major knot—ties together all the strands of the narrative.

It is therefore certain that Grey plotted his work carefully. The idea that a great novel can be written haphazardly or impromptu is ludicrous. As a way of creating a work with tight and logical structure, Grey, as with any writer, must see the end of his work from the beginning. Only then can all the strands of causation and its effects maintain unity, which is the first requirement of the novel.

As Lassiter and Withersteen's relationship develops more depth and intimacy, *Riders'* storyline gathers energy and pace through the actions of Bern Venters.

The structuring of parallel plots allows the narrative greater interest, particularly when the two plots converge toward the end. When one plot slows down, the other can energize the pace. Lassiter as the alpha male tries to fulfill his mission, while Venters in a secondary role adds a more sensitive dimension to the narrative. This "swallowtail plot," as it has come to be known, is handled effortlessly by Zane Grey.

Seeking stolen cattle near Deception Pass, Venters encounters Oldring's Masked Rider—actually Bess Oldring in disguise. This scene, as Venters shoots the Masked Rider and discovers it is a woman, turns histrionic. But for readers in 1912 and thereafter it was tender and romantic. Wounded by Venters, Bess survives. The two enter Surprise Valley, an Edenic blind canyon whose entry is guarded by the massive Balancing Rock. Dislodging the rock would send it tumbling down, sealing the valley forever. The rock becomes one of the focal points of the novel. Venters and Lassiter are always mindful of its sinister presence. For centuries it has rested on a square foot of sandstone at the mercy of rain and wind. The ancient peoples have revered it like a god, always aware that its plunge down the hillside might spell doom for their existence.

Similarly, the major characters in the novel—Withersteen, Lassiter, Venters, Bess Oldring, and Tull—are on the edge of their own cliffs, where any wrong turn or split decision will send them careening into tragedy. At one point, Lassiter, upon seeing Balanced Rock, tells Venters: "I always had the funniest notion to roll stones! When I was a kid I did it, an' the bigger I got the bigger stones I'd roll. Ain't that funny? Honest—even now I often get off a hoss just to tumble a big stone over a precipice, en' watch it drop, an' listen to it bang and boom. I've started

(4-1) WEIRD AND WONDERFUL MONUMENTS IN MONUMENT VALLEY

Traveling through Monument Valley opened a whole new world to Zane.

some slides in my time an' don't you forget it. I never seen a rock I wanted to roll as bad as this one. Wouldn't there jest be roarin', crashin' hell down that trail?"[9]

Revealing his sensitive, protective nature, Venters cares for Bess and nurtures her to health. While she recovers, he investigates the mysteries of Surprise Valley, which contains a vast hive of cliff dwellings left by ancient Indians.

At this point in the Venters-Bess plot, it is not difficult to imagine that the attentive cowboy is reminiscent of the adventurous Zane Grey. As Grey had scrambled over Indian ruins in northern Arizona and southern Utah, Venters casts his eyes on these remote dusty tombs.

"This place," Grey writes, "was of proportions that stunned [Venters], and it had not been desecrated by the hand of man, nor had it been crumbled by the hand of time. It was a stupendous tomb. It had been a city. It was just as it had been left by its builders. The little houses were there, the smoke-blackened stains of fire. . . . But the cliff-dwellers were gone!"[10]

Surprise Valley provides Venters and Bess emotional and physical sustenance. Their water and food needs are provided by a nearby spring and the abundant game of the canyon. Venters raids the cliff dwellings for pottery and crocks, hoping to replace his trusty tin cup—used for everything from soup to coffee—with something more artful. Under his care, Bess's health improves daily. She undergoes a minor metamorphosis from fearsome bandit to winsome ladylove. Grey develops this process slowly and believably, as the sheer walls of Surprise Valley begin to comfort them both. Grey writes: "Day by day Venters watched the white of her face slowly change to brown and the wasted cheeks fill out by imperceptible degrees. . . . Many times Venters found the clear gaze embarrassing to him, yet, like wine, it had an exhilarating effect. What did she think when she looked at him so? Almost he believed she had no thought at all. All about her and the present there in Surprise Valley, and the dim yet subtly impending future, fascinated Venters and made him thoughtful as all his lonely vigils in the sage had not."[11]

As love begins to tug at his heart, Venters often regrets the passing days that anticipate the time they must leave the valley and return to

Keet Seel ruins near Kayenta, Arizona, provided Zane Grey a basis for his study of ancient cliff dwellers.

civilization. Grey notes that Venters "began to think of improving Surprise Valley as a place to live in."[12]

Grey could have sped through this plot strand, but to his credit he lets Venters and Bess's relationship unfold naturally. Under Venters's tutelage, Bess awakens to a fresh new world. She wonders about the people who lived in the canyon centuries ago and asks Venters who they were.

"Cliff dwellers," Venters explains. "Men who had enemies and made their home high out of reach."

"They had to fight? . . . For—what?"

"For life. For their homes, food, children, parents—for their women!"[13]

Bess is torn between leaving the canyon and staying where they are. "I want to go out into the big world and see it," she tells Venters. "Yet I want to stay here more. What is to become of us? Are we cliff dwellers?"[14]

At this point in the storyline, readers might surmise that the Bern Venters–Bess Oldring plot is just a nice cozy romance in the midst of an arcadian setting. It isn't until the end of the novel that this strand of the plot makes any sense in the unity of the narrative.

Against their immediate wishes, they cannot stay in the canyon. The outside world, it would appear, is too much with them. There are villains to punish, outlaws to subdue, secrets to unlock, knots to untie—and, presumably, clothes to launder.

But before they can reach a final decision, Bess makes a surprising find in a stream in the canyon. "Gold!" cries Venters. This rapid change in fortune—the novel's peripety—allows Bess and Bern to plan their futures, a decision, it turns out, that sends the narrative in a new direction.

* * *

Grey was one of the first writers to use the transition "Meantime, at the ranch," which appears at the beginning of chapter 6. It, of course, has become such a shopworn catchphrase that no one dare use it again—in speech or in writing. As the story shifts back to Lassiter and Withersteen, Jane visits the southern, Gentile section of the town of Cottonwoods. She visits the dying Mrs. Larkin, who agrees to let Jane raise her seven-year-old daughter, Fay, after the ailing woman has died. Fay wiggles into the arms and heart of Jane and Lassiter. The gunslinger, in particular, finds Fay

Navajo hogans in northern Arizona

irresistible. It isn't long before Lassiter is smitten by Jane and Fay and has left toiling as Jane's rider on the purple sage and begun clinking his spurs on the floors of her house. Jane still yearns to take Lassiter's guns, fearing that he will kill any Mormon who walks through the door. And two Mormons in particular, Bishop Dyer and Elder Tull, trouble her dreams.

Ranch life turns disastrous for Jane. Her cattle have been rustled; several of her riders have left the estate; her beloved horses have vanished. Even her beloved equines, Black Star and Night, are stolen by Oldring's gang. After a fierce chase, Venters returns Jane's horses and goes in search of Oldring and his sponsors: Tull and Dyer.

Chapter 18 contains some masterful writing—indeed, Zane Grey at his best. Readers and critics have always admired his ability with description, but this is only a part of Grey's skill. Like many writers before him, such as Henry James and George Eliot, he allowed his characters to wrestle with their own inner turmoil and guilt. He packed paragraphs with emotional electricity, so that the characters emerged with all their flaws revealed in brilliant plumage.

In the following scene Venters rides into the town of Cottonwoods and seeks revenge on Oldring, whose abusive treatment of Bess has enraged the cowboy. Venters encounters Oldring in the saloon and goads him into a gunfight outside. Oldring kicks a chair, bolts out of the saloon, and stands before his adversary: "Venters had one glimpse of his great breadth and bulk, his gold-buckled belt and hanging guns, his high-top boots with gold spurs. . . . his whole splendid presence so wonderfully charged with vitality and force and strength, seemed to afford Venters an unutterable fiendish joy because for that magnificent manhood and life he meant cold and sudden death." After Venters shoots Oldring, the rustler mutters something unintelligible just before expiring.[15]

Venters flees town and heads for Surprise Valley, his body aching from exertion, his mind reeling from strain. Grey resumes: "He suffered without understanding why. He caught glimpses into himself, into unlit darkness of soul. The fire that had blistered him and the cold which had frozen him now united in one torturing possession of his mind and heart, and like a fiery steed with ice-shod feet, ranged his being, ran rioting through his blood, trampling the resurging good, dragging ever at the evil."[16]

Venters rests in his mission to see Bess, and through the fog of his memory, he tries to understand the meaning of Oldring's dying words. "What a look in the eyes of a man shot through the heart! . . . Venters saw in Oldring's magnificent eyes the rolling of great, glad surprise—softness—love! Then came a shadow and the terrible superhuman striving of his spirit to speak. Oldring, shot through the heart, hand fought and forced back death, not for a moment in which to short or curse, but to whisper strange words."[17]

Only later do we learn, during the untying of the major knot, that Bess Oldring is actually the daughter of Lassiter's sister, Milly Erne, and her proper name is Elizabeth Erne. In the novel, Bess has four identities, three of which are false: Masked Rider, outlaw, Oldring's daughter, and Milly's child. The mixed identities plot has a solid pedigree, from Restoration drama to the romanticists of the nineteenth and early twentieth centuries.

The next unmasking of a character involves Jane Withersteen. Since Lassiter's arrival at Cottonwoods, Jane has kept a secret from the gunman, a secret that she feels would doom her relationship with him. On the brink of this breakup, she admits that it was her father, together with Bishop Dyer, who lured Milly Erne from her home and brought her to Utah. It was Dyer, Jane confesses, who abducted Milly's daughter, Elizabeth Erne, and handed her to Oldring to engage in a criminal life. The outlaw had tried to protect Bess but had incurred the animosity of the Mormon bishop as a result.

Lassiter forgives Jane and swears his love for her. In a frenzied scene, Lassiter shoots and kills Dyer. He would have also slain Tull, but the elder was out with his riders. Realizing that her church community is closing in on her, Jane tells Lassiter she will ride away with him. "Hide me till danger is past—till we are forgotten—then take me where you will. Your people shall be my people, and your God my God!"[18]

The storyline knot, which Grey has tied unmercifully tight, begins to unravel. What has been resolved? Lassiter fulfills his quest, uncovers secrets, and wins Jane's heart; Jane endures the anger of a hostile community, adopts young Fay, and prepares to leave her beloved Cottonwoods ranch. Her emotional and psychological journey from distressed young heiress to confident, courageous woman is one of the highlights of the novel.

Bern Venters escapes the wrath of the Mormons, discovers a valley of gold, unmasks an outlaw, kills Oldring, and finds a way home. Bess Oldring—Elizabeth Erne—flees a repressive and criminal life, discovers romance, learns her true identity, and finds a new family.

After their misdeeds, Elder Tull and Bishop Dyer meet their separate ends: Tull is thwarted by Lassiter and Withersteen; Dyer meets a violent end at the hands of Lassiter. With Oldring, Tull, and Dyer out of the way, the once malicious Mormon community can return to some normalcy.

The narrative then settles into its resolution, or denouement (a French term that literally means "to untie"). Threatened by an enraged Tull and his riders, Jane leaps on Black Star and makes her getaway. Grey writes, "She rode out of the court . . . through the grove, across the wide lane into the sage, and she realized that she was leaving Withersteen House forever, and she did not look back. A strange, dreamy, calm peace pervaded her soul. Her doom had fallen upon her, but instead of finding life no longer worth living she found it doubly significant, full of sweetness as the western breeze, beautiful and unknown as the sage-slope stretching its purple sunset shadows before her."[19]

Lassiter sets Withersteen House afire. Astride Night, Lassiter catches up to Jane and rides beside her. They both gallop toward Surprise Valley, Tull's gang a short distance behind them. Thick, billowing clouds of smoke trail in their wake as the house shrivels into scorched timbers.

Along the trail to Deception Pass, they meet Venters and Bess, who are fleeing Surprise Valley and heading east to Illinois. After a brief meeting between the couples, Venters and Bess head north, while Lassiter and Jane steer toward the valley.

In his brilliant conclusion to the story, Grey involves both Jane and Lassiter in the decision to roll Balancing Rock and seal the entrance to Surprise Valley. The badly wounded gunfighter tells Jane he cannot roll the stone. "Why? Haven't you the strength left . . . ?" cries Jane.

"Jane—it ain't that—I've lost my nerve! . . . I wanted to roll it—meant to—but I—can't. Venters's valley is down behind here. We could—live there. But if I roll the stone—we're shut in for always. I don't dare. I'm thinkin' of you!"

As Tull and his men approach from below, Jane shouts: "Roll the stone! . . . Lassiter, I love you!"

Presently, Lassiter consents, braces his shoulder against the rock, and sends it hurtling down the chasm.[20]

* * *

Although Zane Grey's narrative contains most of the elements of romance and melodrama combined with simply implausible coincidences, it is a story that defined and invigorated the Western genre for several years to come. While many readers consider these aspects too fanciful, innumerable critics of the genre find them fascinating, particularly when they are reshaped in the mind of a good writer. Most of the features described in *Riders of the Purple Sage*, simply speaking, were found in the plethora of dime novels at the end of the nineteenth century. Except for the hackneyed idioms and language and the gaudy clothes of the central characters, the fundamental qualities of the Western genre have not changed in over a hundred years.

The concept of Surprise Valley came as no real surprise to readers of early Western tales featuring El Dorados, buried treasure, and lost gold mines. But a canyon guarded by a balancing rock was a novel idea that Grey took advantage of. By the end of the nineteenth century and the beginning of the twentieth, romanticist writers were exploiting the diminishing areas of the world that were devoid of human contact. Lost worlds where civilizations once flourished became the material of fictioneers in England, Germany, and France. Celebrated romanticists of these exotic locales forgotten by time included H. Rider Haggard (*King Solomon's Mines*), W. H. Hudson (*Green Mansions*), and Sir Arthur Conan Doyle (*The Lost World*), whose work of fiction was published the same year as *Riders of the Purple Sage*. A young writer who survived Grubstreet, Edgar Rice Burroughs, gained fame with his *Tarzan of the Apes*, also published in 1912.

These authors imagined a world secluded from the evils of modern society and a paradise once inhabited by a noble race. In the footsteps of these writers, and quite possibly stimulated by them, Grey carved out his own arcadia in the isolated high desert of Arizona.

A strong work of fiction needs memorable character names, and *Riders* possesses them in abundance. Grey worked over his character names during the first draft of each book. He wrote them down and reworked their spellings, hoping to find the right sound for the right personality. In accordance with the times, Western characters had first and last names. Later in the century, characters with one name (Hondo or Shane) became popular, until "the man with no name" appeared. But each character's name had to reflect his or her core personality as well as register forcefully in the mind of the reader.

Grey avoided becoming silly with certain names and concentrated on those names that sounded and functioned well: Jim Lassiter, Jane Withersteen, Bern Venters, Elizabeth Erne, Oldring, Tull, Dyer. Lassiter is perhaps the best name of a Western gunman in the genre—strong, noble, persistent, steadfast, and tough. His name lingers like gun smoke on a still day. Jane Withersteen is also a splendid name for Grey's heroine, reflecting her noble but not arrogant heritage. Grey may have based the name on Thomas Hardy's lead character, Bathsheba Everdeen, in *Far from the Madding Crowd.* Their gutsy personalities are so similar, as is the ring of their last names. In *Riders,* the two central characters' last names have three syllables, while the others have two, or one in some cases. Grey had to invent names that rang true but were not too contrived or foolish sounding. They also had to be distinctive from each other for the reader to differentiate the characters.

Grey mastered the art of naming his characters, and far beyond the world of *Riders of the Purple Sage,* he continued this tradition in novel after novel.

CHAPTER EIGHT

After the Rainbow

WHEN ZANE VISITED FRANKLIN SQUARE IN THE EARLY DAYS OF 1913, Hitchcock and Duneka had a bundle of fan mail for him. At first he was shocked and amused. He was not expecting such a response from readers who had followed Lassiter and Venters through all the trails and canyons in *Riders of the Purple Sage*. A few were eager to know what became of the gunfighter and Jane during their sojourn in Surprise Valley. Others remarked that the novel had ended too soon.

As time went on, the background noise surrounding the fate of Jane and Lassiter grew louder. People stopped Grey on the street in New York and asked him for details; others greeted him at the Weatherford Hotel and cornered him about the prospect of a sequel. But for the time being, at least, he was content that the novel had earned him $50,000 in 1912, and it appeared that it would at least equal that amount in 1913. Grey had turned over to Harper and Brothers his new novels, *Desert Gold* and *The Light of Western Stars*, which were soon to be serialized in *Popular* magazine, beginning May 1913. He simply was in no position to begin thinking of rescuing the characters of *Riders of the Purple Sage*.

He and Dolly were now the parents of Romer Grey (born 1909) and Betty Zane Grey (born 1912). They had remodeled the house in Lacka-waxen and hired domestic help. The Greys also bought a house in Middle-town, New York, which they resided in periodically and which featured less frigid winters. From November to March in any year, Grey chained himself to his writing desk and poured out his narratives. When April came, he was off on the Santa Fe Railroad to points west. In spring 1913 he was headed to Kayenta, Arizona, to rendezvous with John Wetherill.

His goal was to travel overland to the Rainbow Bridge, now a landmark attraction for professional as well as amateur explorers.

Dolly tolerated most of Zane's absences, realizing that his travels alleviated many of the black moods that sent him into unsettling hibernations or periodic rages. The sound of the train whistle and the rumble of rails raised Grey's joy for living immeasurably. By the second decade of the twentieth century, Dolly was sufficiently schooled in Grey's routines that a trip west meant he was happy and she could be relieved of trying to nurse him. Besides, she could edit his next manuscript or engage in activities that she liked, namely corresponding with relatives in Europe and raising her children.

Whether at home or on the road, Grey was averaging close to 25,000 to 35,000 words per month—a frenzied pace for even the most veteran novelist. He could write for seven hours straight, seven days a week. When a novel was nearing completion, he could barrel through by pulling ten- to twelve-hour shifts at his desk or chair. This pace resulted in one novel per year, sometimes two. His literary success was now certain, but he wished to sustain it for as long as it took.

After spending a few days in Kayenta with Wetherill, Grey began to conceive of a sequel to *Riders of the Purple Sage*. By this time he had developed a pattern for his Western storylines. A typical plot from this period has an emotionally wounded hero, usually from the East, who travels west for some type of restoration. The hero sometimes rescues a woman from dirty dealings in her sphere, pulling the hero into a situation that requires him to rise above his limitations. Although many of the plots are set in different locales and time periods, the pattern was usually consistent. Harper's managers, aware that they had one of the most bankable authors in America, loosened the reins on their middlebrow author, since he was generating more income than several of their more established authors.

Accompanying Grey on this exploration of the Rainbow Bridge was Dolly's thirty-year-old cousin, Lillian Wilhelm, a highly talented artist by anyone's measure. Born in Germany in 1882 but raised and schooled in New York City, Wilhelm had first honed her skills at Buffalo Bill's Wild West show in 1907. Zane had escorted her there, and her experience transformed her from a timid graduate of the New York Academy of

Zane on his horse, Don Carlos, in the Tonto Forest, Arizona, in 1918

Design and the Art Students League into a first-rate painter of Indians and cowboys of the Wild West. When she heard that Zane was considering a sequel to *Riders of the Purple Sage*, she lobbied Dolly for the chance to join his retinue in northern Arizona, in hopes of illustrating the kind of book the author had in mind. By this time, however, she had to compete with a cadre of fine illustrators in New York, including Douglas Duer, W. H. D. Koerner, Herbert Buck Dunton, Frank Tenney Johnson, and N. C. Wyeth. For an artist to be in their league required some serious talent.

Lillian usually tagged around with another cousin of Dolly, Elma Swartz. The two were relatively footloose sorts who enjoyed excursions with Zane Grey. At first, Dolly thought that the relationship between Zane and these women was simply friendly and platonic, but as time went on she realized that her marriage was threatened. Zane's emotional immaturity had become obsessive, and these women offered their veneration of his fame and talents.

Lillian was unmarried, somewhat attractive, slender, and bold as brass, which made her the envy of Dolly Grey. Wilhelm, like Zane, loved the salubrious bite of the desert air, the intense blue of the sky, and the lonely hairpin trails that meandered over the slanting rock faces. She, in truth, loved everything that Zane Grey loved and that Dolly tended to avoid. Dolly was housebound with two young children to care for, while her cousins were out west with her husband. What was a spouse to do?

Dolly, grudgingly perhaps, agreed to the 1913 outing in the Southwest. At this time the Grey marriage showed signs of stress and turmoil. Cracks in the marriage had been showing for several years, but now as he departed with Lillian and Elma, Dolly felt bitterness at being the stable, longsuffering spouse. Dolly had raised the idea that she might like to go with him on this occasion, but Zane refused her offer. "But I don't want you," Zane bluntly told her. In her diary Dolly unleashed her rage: "Why do I put up with these things? Part of the answer, I suppose, is that I care for my husband, that he cannot help these things. They are terrible obsessions with him. He lives in a world of emotion." Toward the end of her entry, she noted: "Doc is a dreamer, a smiler, an intense egotist. In the same breath he can tell me that it's agony for him to leave me and the

children and then that he can't keep from the things in N.Y. Very frankly
he tells me that when he's miserable or sick or needs help, he comes home,
but his good times he likes with the others." Despite her resentment, she
concluded that "for better or worse I must stick to him."[1]

To most observers and family members, such a precarious relationship could not last, but Dolly was not a usual woman. She cared for his
welfare—yes, she loved his charm, and yes, she admired his boyish, Huck
Finn irresponsibility; she may, in a strange way, have even liked him being
out with other women, supplying him with energy and admiration she
could not give him herself.

Wherever they went, especially in the West, Lillian and Elma talked
and behaved in the manner they wanted. They rejected many of the conventions of the time. Upon arriving in Flagstaff with Zane, they prepared
their horses for the long ride to Kayenta. Lillian viewed the landscape
before her: "I was initiated into my life in this blessed land by a four-
hundred-mile horseback trip, accompanied by a chuck wagon full of supplies," she wrote a few years later. "We left Flagstaff to penetrate into the
shimmering beauty of the Painted Desert region. . . . Our dear old guide,
Al Doyle, who showed me how to ride like a cowboy so that the long
twenty-five and thirty miles that constituted the day's loping and trot-
ting would not tire me, showed me to a place at the end of the day where
I could paint, and try—and oh how I tried—sometimes to the point of
tears—to interpret the divine beauty of those sunsets."[2]

As they made their way to the Wetherills' trading post in Kayenta,
Lillian sensed that her destiny lay before her. Most New York illustrators
of Western works had not been beyond the Mississippi River. A few, like
Frederic Remington twenty or so years earlier, had made their fortunes by
depicting the denizens and landscapes of the Southwest. The fact that she
was woman in a man's world did not affect her—in fact, it drove her on.

The Wetherills always tried to accommodate the wayfarer as well as
the serious archaeologist. But it was no secret that John Wetherill preferred to guide science professionals because tourists tended to dillydally
too much along the way. Later in the year they would welcome former
president Theodore Roosevelt for his trip to the Rainbow Bridge. Roosevelt was still smarting from his Bull Moose Party's loss to Woodrow

Flagstaff, Arizona, became one of Zane's important destinations for travels in the Southwest.
FRANKBACH @SHUTTERSTOCK.COM

Wilson a year earlier, only to suffer blistering saddle sores on his trek into southern Utah. After Roosevelt came and went, two famous Grand Canyon photographers—the Kolb brothers, Ellsworth and Emery—joined Wetherill for a pack mule trip on the Rainbow Trail.

After consulting Grey, Wetherill planned to head north to Monument Valley, then begin looping to the southeast and visit Betatakin and Keet Seel ruins before steering to Tsegi Canyon, where they would briefly rest. The journey would continue on the Rainbow Trail to the monumental bridge across the Arizona border. Lillian and Elma would remain at the trading post and then meet them on the return journey with the supply wagon. In addition to Grey, Wetherill's scouting party included Joe Lee, a bowlegged Mormon rancher. After a time they picked up one of the best Paiute Indian guides, Nasja Begay, who would take them over Navajo Mountain and down to the Rainbow Bridge. In Navajo the formation is called Tsnnaa Nanizhoozi (rock span); Grey spelled it Nonnezoshe. But regardless of language, it was the holy grail of Southwestern treasures in the early part of the century.

The Monument Valley loop was meant to accommodate Zane Grey. Approaching the valley, Grey found "a world of colossal shafts and buttes of rock, magnificently sculptured, standing isolated and aloof, dark, weird, and lonely."[3] Grey sat on horseback, watching flashes of lightning forking over the buttes. "It was hard for me to realize," quipped Zane, "that those monuments were not the work of man. The great valley must once have been in a plateau of red rock from which the softer strata had eroded, leaving the gentle, league-long slopes marked here and there by upstanding pillars and columns of singular shape and beauty."[4]

They turned south toward Tsegi Canyon (Surprise Valley in *Riders*) near Marsh Pass, where Zane was overcome with nostalgia for the place and his exiled characters, Jim Lassiter and Jane Withersteen. "Something of awe and sadness abided with me," he remarked. "Surprise Valley seemed a part of my past, my dreams, my very self."[5] He also speculated about a way to free his heroine and hero from the clutches of this walled and pillared paradise. His fleeting thoughts soon turned into the words that would become his next novel.

Sagebrush, sand, and buttes of Monument Valley, Arizona

The most arduous part of the journey lay ahead. Soon they met their Southern Paiute guide, a veteran of the 1909 Cummings-Douglass expedition. Nasja Begay (Son of Owl) was a half, perhaps a full, inch shorter than Grey. He wore his jet-black hair in braided tails or loose on his forehead. He had dark skin, creased like parchment, that bore signs of sun, wind, and rain. He wore a faded wool shirt and durable moccasins.

The guide spoke in broken English or Ute, preferring to communicate in common gestures that showed directions or time of day. When necessary, he could converse with Wetherill in Navajo, which for many white settlers was near impossible to learn. Grey came to admire his stealth and endurance. "There is always something so significant and impressive about an Indian when he points anywhere," the author remarked.[6]

The disjointed caravan poked along. It would be difficult to imagine a more colorful group of travelers in the Old West: Wetherill in the lead, his horse nodding forward; Nasja Begay riding beside him, looking at the sky and horizon; Joe Lee, a comfortable distance behind, his eyes sometimes drifting to sleep; Grey soaking it all in—the colors, shapes, and several orphan clouds.

Fortunately, they were free of inclement weather. In April and May of any given year the wind and rain can sweep down over the mesas, causing the gulches to flood and overwhelm their banks. The sun rose on their right flank, burned like a cinder at noon, and set as a pale, red wafer into the inky twilight. After they reached a promontory, Grey joined Wetherill and stared at the vista before them. Wetherill pointed north.

"You can see two hundred miles into Utah," Wetherill said. "That bright surface, like a washboard, is wind-worn rock. Those little lines of cleavage are canyons. There are a thousand canyons down there, and only a few have we been in. That long purple ragged line is the Grand Canyon of the Colorado. And there, that blue fork in the red, that's where the San Juan comes in. And there's Escalante Canyon."[7]

Zane stared, his sweeping gaze passing over the pillars and mesas. "I imagined," Grey confessed, "that there was no scene in all the world to equal this. The tranquility of lesser spaces was here not manifest. This happened to be a place where so much of the desert could be seen and the effect was stupendous. Sound, movement, life seemed to have no fitness here. Ruin was there and desolation and decay. The meaning of the ages was flung at me. A man became nothing."[8]

On the northwestern side of Navajo Mountain they encountered a maze of canyons, one of them leading to the mouth of the gulch holding the Rainbow Bridge. Presently, they stood in front of it, and Grey reported that it "absolutely silenced me. My body and brain, weary and dull from the toil of travel, received a singular and revivifying freshness. I had a strange mystic perception that this rosy-hued, tremendous arch of stone was a goal I had failed to reach in some former life, but had now found. Here was a rainbow magnified even beyond dreams, a thing not transparent and ethereal, but solidified, a work of ages, sweeping up majestically from the red walls, its iris-hued arch against the blue sky."[9]

That night they camped under the soaring arch. At dawn, as the sun transformed the shadowed arc into a pastel rainbow, Grey reflected: "Long before life had evolved upon the earth this bridge had spread its grand arch from wall to wall, black and mystic at night, transparent and rosy in the sunrise, at sunset a flaming curve limned against the heavens."[10]

They had traveled over one hundred miles through some of the most rugged, hazardous, and forbidding country in America. But under the shadow of the bridge, Grey felt rested and at home.

Serenity for Zane Grey meant completion of the journey, any journey. The great monuments of the West—the Grand Canyon, Keet Seel, Canyon de Chelly, Chaco Canyon, Escalante Plateau, and Nonnezoshe—had more significance for him than the temples, cathedrals, and holy shrines of Europe. The Rainbow Bridge was handcrafted in America by God, a span linking ancient peoples to modern-day pilgrims, a symbol of the permanence of nature, and a site honored by millions but witnessed by the very few.

As for his companions on the trek, Nasja Begay became Nas ta Bega, and John Wetherill reappeared in the character of Withers in *The Rainbow Trail*. Lillian Wilhelm also endured, providing Grey inspiration on two occasions: as the dark-haired Indian Mescal in *The Heritage of the Desert*, and as the malleable protagonist Madeline "Majesty" Hammond in *The Light of Western Stars* (1914). In the latter novel, the spirited socialite Majesty travels west and finds the love of a rangy, good-natured

Zane Grey, lower left, beneath the Rainbow Bridge in 1913

cowboy named Gene Stewart. Like other Grey heroes, she arrives in New Mexico as an empty vessel: "She had been assailed by a great weariness, an ice-sickening sense that life had palled upon her. She was tired of fashionable society. She was tired of polished and imperturbable men who sought only to please her. She was tired of being feted, admired, loved, and importuned; tired of people; tired of houses, noise, ostentation, luxury. She was so tired of herself!"[11]After scanning the horizon she admits that "she knew what she needed—to be alone, to brood for long hours, to gaze out on lonely, silent, darkening stretches, to watch the stars, to face her soul, to find her real self."[12] Like his portrayal of Majesty Hammond, Grey's women friends were expected to be poised, well-educated, and brave enough to face some adversity. They were women like his ancestor Betty Zane: smart and pretty, but able to carry an apron full of ammunition through a hail of bullets.

Lillian Wilhelm fit this model. She remained friendly with the Greys throughout the years. After returning from the Rainbow Bridge excursion, she sold a few paintings to Harper to accompany Grey's novel. Eventually, the publisher used her portrayal of the Rainbow Bridge as the frontispiece. She later illustrated Grey's *The Border Legion*. At this time, she wed the financier Westbrooke Robertson, but the marriage was unhappy and they divorced in 1924. Like Majesty Hammond she looked for a mate unpossessed by wealth and social standing, and found him in Jesse Smith, an easygoing cowboy who advised Grey on Western movie details. "Jess" was the brother of Grey's secretary, Mildred Smith. Lillian moved permanently to Arizona and at various times lived in Scottsdale, Sedona, and Prescott. As a pioneer woman painter, she created some of the best Southwestern landscapes of the early part of the century.

In addition to Lillian and Elma, various other women, whom Grey often called his "secretaries," entered and retreated from his life. Throughout the 1920s and into the next decade, as his career skyrocketed, Zane and Dolly went through periods of extreme bliss followed by bouts of anger, resentment, and threats of divorce. Zane was frequently absent, while Dolly raised two children under five years old. In one letter she wondered if she had "any moral backbone" to stand up to him. "Oh my God, I'm too young and full of life to have to settle down and find my only happiness in my children. I need more. If only I could—but I can't. I'm younger now than I was ten years ago."[13]

* * *

Since the turn of the century, Frank Munsey had built his publishing empire into one of the mightiest in New York City. *Popular*, *Munsey's*, and *Argosy*, to name a few magazines, had become household names, featuring some of the best and upcoming writers in America. Zane Grey had become one of the most sought-after writers by magazine editors, in an age when serializations of books were almost standard practice in publishing.

Helming the staff at these magazines was Bob Davis, who had learned from his mistake of rejecting *Riders of the Purple Sage* for serialization in one of Munsey's magazines. The penitent Davis was now eager to run a Grey story—most any story from the Western writer's pen. In March 1913, *Popular* issued *Desert Gold*; in May 1913, *Munsey's* published *The Light of Western Stars*. When Grey approached Davis with the manuscript for *The Desert Crucible* in late 1914, the editor prepared it for publication in *Argosy*, beginning in May of the following year. By now Grey was so famous that Eltinge Warner at *Field and Stream* nearly begged the author to run the novel several months later. Harper and Brothers allowed this preemptive move on the part of the magazines because it afforded them pre-publication publicity, which generally boosted book sales in the future.

In winter 1914, Grey sent the long-awaited sequel to *Riders of the Purple Sage* to *Argosy* and to Harper for editing. Bob Davis made a small number of changes and issued it under Grey's original title, *The Desert Crucible*. In contrast, Harper took a more careful approach.

Duneka and Hitchcock, along with several senior editors, were anticipating another successful Grey title, but the specter associated with *Riders of the Purple Sage* appeared once again. First, the editors decided the title was not appropriate for the theme of the book, so Hitchcock suggested that *The Rainbow Trail* would attract more readers. Once the title was agreed upon, their attention was fixed on the text.

Once again, Frederick Duneka was faced with an unsettling decision. He could make some cuts in the manuscript he felt were necessary and risk offending Zane Grey. *The Rainbow Trail* was even more hostile to Mormons than *Riders* and more explicit in its condemnation of arranged marriages. Grey's latest novel included scenes of an LDS village in northern Arizona where Mormon men periodically visited their sealed wives. Moreover, the scenes generated high degrees of sexual energy among the characters.

Duneka was at the same time involved in preparing Mark Twain's posthumous novel, *The Mysterious Stranger*, for publication, a book patched together from three separate manuscripts. He and Albert Bigelow Paine had the best of intentions. They wanted to present Twain's novel in a form acceptable to their readership, but Duneka went one step further. Many years later it was discovered that the Harper's manager had added several pages to the novel that he himself had written. In trying to make the manuscript more cohesive, he had created a scarlet literary sin. These pages written by Duneka were in addition to the cuts made in Twain's manuscript regarding the defects of organized religion. Harper's bowdlerized version was published in 1916, a few months after Grey's novel was issued.

Similarly, Duneka wanted to present a more sanitized version of *The Rainbow Trail*. Censored and expurgated editions of novels and plays were not new. In 1807, Thomas Bowdler, an English physician, published the first edition of *The Family Shakespeare*, which made available the Bard's plays for women and children. Bowdler's work appeared in several editions over the years, eventually lending his name to any work edited for certain content. Over the years, many authors have had their works bowdlerized or outright censored for sexual, ethnic, or religious reasons. Censorship usually involves banning the entire book, which has happened to several authors, including D. H. Lawrence and James Joyce in the early twentieth century. Expurgation is the selective removal of certain passage deemed offensive to current public tastes.

Harper's editors zeroed in on references to Mormon men having excessive numbers of children with plural wives. In one case in *The Rainbow Trail*, a Mormon husband with five wives and fifty-five children makes periodic visits to the home of the book's heroine, whom he considers his sealed wife.[14] Polygamy was one thing, but such behavior with the hero's love interest was quite another. Duneka had these sections cut, and they did not appear in book form until the early 2000s, when the private corporation Zane Grey Inc. reissued the novel under Grey's original title, *The Desert Crucible*. But as far as expurgations go, *The Rainbow Trail* was only sparingly trimmed.

After Grey agreed to the revisions, Hitchcock forged ahead to the novel's publication date, secure in the knowledge that his author was approaching stardom.

*   *   *

After the changes, *The Desert Crucible*, more widely known as *The Rainbow Trail*, was published by Harper and Brothers in September 1915. It is a fitting sequel to *Riders of the Purple Sage*, even though its pace is more sluggish and its plot less complex. Further, it is the most autobiographical of all Grey's early novels, and nearly approaches an allegory of the author's life in the Southwest. Most of the events in *The Rainbow Trail* follow closely Grey's excursion to the Rainbow Bridge with John Wetherill in 1913. The novel was written during a period of increased tension in the Grey marriage. Although Zane and Dolly were anticipating their ten-year anniversary in November 1915, Dolly had little cause for celebration. Zane was enduring his own crucible by trying to reconcile his wanderings and dalliances with the need for a stable married life. This tension often reveals itself in the relationships of the novel.

The setting for the novel is the Arizona Territory circa 1883, ten years after the events in *Riders of the Purple Sage*. A man—a defrocked pastor—has come to northern Arizona to find the whereabouts of Lassiter, Jane, and young Fay Larkin. But it is the image of Fay, now nearly twenty years old, that lures him on. After a brief stop in Flagstaff he heads north, at first aimlessly, then with a dogged persistence in finding his way to Kayenta, the wayfarers' rest and the home of a trader named Withers. He travels north to the Little Colorado River and encounters the landscape of the northern desert: "Like ocean waves the slope rose and fell, its hollows choked with sand, its ridge-tops showing scantier growth of sage and grass and weed. The last ridge was a sand-dune, beautifully ribbed and scalloped and lined by the wind, and from its knife-sharp crest a thin, wavering sheet of sand blew, almost like smoke."[15]

The prelude to this pilgrimage begins months earlier in Illinois. The man, John Shefford, is twenty-four years old and a seeker by anyone's definition. As the pastor of a church, he has mentored Bern Venters and Elisabeth Erne and learned of the Utah events involving Jim Lassiter, Jane, Fay, and Surprise Valley. Over time, the fate of young Fay becomes an obsession for him. As he moves further and further away from church doctrine and begins questioning the existence of God, his congregation turns on him and forces him out. Demoralized and full of self-loathing, he heads to Arizona to complete his quest for the truth of the Lassiter family—and to seek his own redemption. Withers tells him outright: "Shefford, go to the Navajo for a faith."[16]

This setting forms the backdrop for Shefford's desert crucible, and what he finds, both among people and in the natural landscape, will test his courage, his faith in humanity, and his belief in God. As in *Riders*, some of the more controversial aspects of Mormonism are part of the tense atmosphere in the novel. The federal authorities have cracked down on polygamy in southern Utah and particularly on husbands with sealed wives. To alleviate this situation, some Mormons have fled to a village in northern Arizona, just across the Utah border, and created a community of plural marriages and servile brides. According to Mormon tradition, a woman sealed in marriage is bound to her husband and she cannot divorce or remarry. The marriage is confirmed on earth and also sealed in heaven. The village is unnamed and doesn't appear on maps, in an area so remote and rugged that only the hardiest of scouts could find it. It is known, however, to Withers and others in the vicinity of his trading post.

As a protagonist, Shefford is no match for heroics of Jim Lassiter, and this is exactly the way Grey planned it. For one thing, Shefford is created in the image of the author. Shefford is an aspiring artist and, by his own admission, a dreamer. He imagines a new life with Fay as his dream woman, even though she is a thousand miles away and he has never met her. Any man who can find true love from such fantasy is a sentimentalist of the first order. Shefford has fallen into the life of a pastor with no real convictions for doing so. Traveling to Arizona to find Fay is his passage from uncertainty to wisdom. At one point, he tries to explain this strange fascination: "Loss of faith and name did not send me to this wilderness.

The ruins of a trading post in the Navajo Nation

But I had love—love for that lost girl, Fay Larkin. I dreamed about her till I loved her. I dreamed that I would find her, my treasure, at the foot of a rainbow. Dreams! . . . Her spirit is all that keeps me kind and good . . . Always I torture myself with the vain dream that—that she might not be dead. I have never been anything but a dreamer."[17]

Shefford's circle of friends soon includes the crusty trader Withers, a character who stems directly from John Wetherill; the devious Mormon missionary Willetts; and the brawny Mormon cowboy Joe Lake. Nas ta Bega assumes a prominent role as Shefford's devoted Navajo friend and spiritual advisor. Nas ta Bega explains to Shefford that he was stolen from his mother's hogan and "taken to California. They kept me ten years in a mission at San Bernardino and four years in a school. They said my color and my hair were all that was left of the Indian in me, but they could not see my heart. They took fourteen years of my life. They wanted to make me a missionary among my own people, but the white man's ways and his life and his God are not the Indian's. They never can be."[18]

The Navajo's quiet lament is echoed in much of Grey's work. Mormonism and Indian religious beliefs are frequently juxtaposed. They are held up to the blazing sun of experience, and the author continually proclaims the truth of the Navajo deities and decries the merciless effect of unwanted missionaries. They "will not leave the Indian in peace with his own God. *Bi-nai*, brother, the Indian is dying," Nas ta Bega tells Shefford.[19]

In Kayenta, Withers hires Shefford to help him run supply trains to Durango, Colorado, and Monticello, Utah. It is routine work but Shefford willingly endures the desert hardships and enjoys meeting the various people of the region. Withers updates him on the events of earlier years: how Cottonwoods has disappeared, how the Rainbow Bridge has beckoned him, and how Tsegi Canyon appears to be the Surprise Valley sheltering Lassiter and Jane. And then, as if to pique Shefford's interest, Withers speaks of "a village of Mormons' sealed wives . . . perhaps twenty miles from here, and near the Utah line. . . . I'm the only Gentile who knows about it, and I pack supplies every few weeks in to these women. There are perhaps fifty women, mostly young second, third, or fourth wives of Mormons . . . sealed wives. I want you to understand that sealed means *sealed* in all that religion or loyalty can get out of the word." Withers further explains that Mormons in southern Utah cross the border into northern Arizona Territory to "pay secret night visits to their sealed wives across the line in the lonely hidden village."[20]

Lured to this village by Withers' intriguing tale, Shefford and the trader load their supplies on their pack animals and head north. Shefford resumes his journey to find Fay Larkin and, hopefully, to encounter his day of atonement. The land beyond Kayenta changes from the scaly desert floor to mountainous stone ridges. Spring temperatures are mild, but over the pillars of Monument Valley dark, heavy thunderheads can form, dragging their wide and dense curtains of rain.

In the hidden village Shefford finds a mysterious assortment of settlers. "The men appeared mild and quiet, and when not conversing, seemed austere. The repose of the women was only on the surface; underneath he felt their intensity. Especially in many of the younger women, whom he met in the succeeding hour, did he feel this power of restrained emotion." Shefford asks himself if they are happy. After some investigation, he concludes: "They certainly seemed to be happy, far more so than those women who were chasing phantoms. Were they really sealed wives . . . and was this unnatural wifehood responsible for the strange intensity?"[21]

Shefford feels the need to reach out to these repressed women and comfort them in their stony silence. But Withers cautions him not to be too forthright: "Any of these Mormon women may fall in love with you. They can't love their husbands. . . . Religion holds them, not love. And the peculiar thing is this. They're second, third, or fourth wives, all sealed. That means their husbands are old, have picked them out for their youth and physical charms, have chosen the very opposite to their first wives, and then have hidden them here in this lonely hole."[22]

When Shefford ultimately meets a mysterious woman named Mary, or Sego Lily, Grey begins to tie the minor knot in the storyline. Over time, Shefford learns the truth: that this secretive, beautiful woman is in fact Fay Larkin, the woman of his dreams, the survivor of Surprise Valley, and a sealed wife to a notorious Mormon elder named Waggoner. Shefford's quest now turns to a way of freeing Fay from the villainous clutches of Waggoner, a man who visits Fay in the dark of night.

The hidden identities plot became a staple of Western novels and movies. The respectable banker is really the fierce leader of a gang of rustlers; the mild-mannered sheriff is in fact working undercover as a federal judge, and so on. The subterfuges are many and the plot twists are plentiful. The unmasking of Fay leads to the major knot in the storyline: How can Shefford unravel her experiences over the previous twelve years?

At one point Fay briefly explains her past to Shefford and her role in the dilemma she now faces. "Oh, I remember so well," Fay begins. "Even now I dream of it sometimes. I hear the roll and crash of falling rock . . . Uncle Jim took me in his arms and started up the cliff. Mother Jane climbed close after us."[23]

For some odd reason, Grey depicts Jane Withersteen and Jim Lassiter as doddering old fools, even though Jane cannot be more than forty years old and Lassiter no older than fifty-five. Even in 1915—the year of the novel's publication—men and women of these ages were not being consigned to wheelchairs and placed in nursing homes for retired gunfighters and their ladies.

If all this action seems fairly operatic—it is. The narrative plays frequently on the strings of romance and leads the reader into a whirlwind of intrigue, desire, and murder. Shefford and Fay spend hours, "so sweet they stung," planning their lives and probing ways of maneuvering out of the bondage of her marriage. She begs Shefford to keep Waggoner away from her: "If you love me, you will do it." When Shefford wonders how, she responds, "You are a man. Any man would save the woman who loves him from . . . a beast. How would Lassiter do it?"[24]

If Shefford needed some bravery, the mention of Lassiter's name—*the* Lassiter—fires his manhood. One night, as Shefford waits near Fay's cabin, the lustful Waggoner rides in unannounced and bolts through Fay's door. Within earshot of the scene, Shefford remains still, his insides boiling. "That sudden flame seemed to curl and twine and shoot along his veins with blasting force."[25] Fay tries to resist her aggressive intruder. A scuffle follows, and Waggoner ends up dead, a knife in his chest.

Without admitting who the killer is, Shefford and Fay, along with Nas ta Bega, make their escape, intending to head for Surprise Valley and liberate Lassiter and Jane. They head west into canyon country, and after freeing Jane and Lassiter from the fertile canyon, they make their way to the Rainbow Bridge, an object for Shefford of both spiritual desire and wondrous beauty. For Shefford, as for Grey, the magisterial arch is something of a bridge to a newfound spirituality. Looking for his rainbow in the West, he realizes the rock span is both his crock of gold and his path to a new life, one wrapped solidly in the grips of this wild land.

Due west of the famous bridge lies the mighty Colorado River, which before the building of the Glen Canyon Dam roared its way unimpeded from the Rockies in Colorado through the Grand Canyon in Arizona. In 1883, it remained one of the most dangerous arteries in America. The force of its rapids below Echo Cliffs could crack a wooden boat like a walnut shell. Here Shefford, Fay, Lassiter, Jane, and Joe Lee hope to run the rapids to safety across the border into Arizona. For all his restrictions as a romance writer, Grey was an exceptional author of action scenes, particularly when they involved men, horses, and swirling rivers.

Luckily, the group survives, and after several grueling days on the river, they camp on a sandbar at the water's edge. As night falls, Shefford, half asleep, hears the roar of the river: "In the distance it rumbled, low, deep, reverberating, and near at hand it was a thing of mutable mood. It moaned, whined, mocked, and laughed. It had the soul of a devil. . . . its nature was destructive, it harbored no life. Fighting its way through those dead walls, cutting and tearing and wearing, its heavy burden of silt was death, destruction, and decay. A silent river, a murmuring, strange, fierce, terrible, thundering river of the desert! Even in the dark it seemed to wear the hue of blood."[26]

Back on the river, they finally reach Lee's Ferry, where they disembark. Joe Lee and Nas ta Bega leave the group. During the trek, the Navajo confesses he is the one who murdered Waggoner. Now free of any legal repercussions, Shefford and Fay join Lassiter and Jane in seeking a new life in Illinois. They are soon reunited with Venters and Elizabeth, thus ending *The Rainbow Trail*.

The flight from the "village of sealed wives," the long ride to the Rainbow Bridge, and the harrowing trek down the Colorado combine to produce pure escapist romance. The author ensures that before his characters take their bows and head to their mundane lives back east, they encounter virtually every major landmark in the Southwest.

For Zane Grey and his readers, it could not have been otherwise.

* * *

Grey's love for this countryside is undeniable, revealing itself in his vivid depictions of desert, mountain ranges, and canyons. He has long been famous for his incisive knowledge of the places and towns of the Southwest. From the moment he set eyes upon the West, his challenge became obvious. Each monument, landmark, trail, canyon, and Indian ruin was unique. He was forced to develop a vocabulary that distinguished each one and revealed to the reader its singular characteristics. This was no easy task. Romance writers have always prized their ability to describe. Joseph Conrad put it this way: "My task is to make you hear, to make you feel, and to make you see. That is all, and it is everything." Grey realized that novice writers often relied on the descriptions of others rather than use their own observations. The need to depend on other writers and their visions is ultimately destructive. He had to go his own way. Before photography, particularly color photography, became prevalent, the writer and the artist had to depend on firsthand experience if they wanted their visions to be singular and compelling.

In the Southwest, the various landforms pose obstacles for the writer. The Vermillion Cliffs, the Grand Canyon, the Colorado River, the Painted Desert, the Rainbow Bridge, Monument Valley, Keet Seel, and Antelope Canyon vary in size, shape, and color. In color, the red sandstones range from light salmon to dark ochre, from brilliant vermillion to faded crimson. In between the segmented layers lie pockets and bands of buff and buckskin-colored rock. Within the segmented layers, textures vary from jagged, razor-sharp points to polished stones as smooth as human skin. The desert Southwest, which Grey championed, is endlessly beautiful in addition to being difficult to describe.

But it is also true that Zane Grey rarely if ever penned a description in the same way twice. After several novels and narrative adventure stories, any writer might have unconsciously repeated himself. But not with Grey; his mind was so focused on each scene that he developed it using

The swirling and beguiling lines of the Wave in the Vermillion Cliffs, northern Arizona, have enchanted travelers for ages.
FRANCESCO CONTI @SHUTTERTOCK.COM

full sensory description. Here is a descriptive passage of Surprise Valley from *Riders of the Purple Sage*, which demonstrates his ability to narratively capture the countryside:

> *Venters turned out of the gorge, and suddenly paused stock-still, astounded at the scene before him. The curve of the great stone bridge had caught the sunrise, and through the magnificent arch burst a glorious stream of gold that shone with a long slant down into the center of Surprise Valley....*
>
> *Down, down, down Venters strode, more and more feeling the weight of his burden as he descended ... At length he passed beyond the slope of weathered stone that spread fan-shape from the arch, and encountered a grassy terrace running to the right.... Silver spruces bordered the base of a precipitous wall that rose loftily....*
>
> *He caught himself often, as he kept busy round the camp-fire, stopping to glance at the quiet form in the cave, and the dogs stretched cozily near him, and then out across the beautiful valley....*
>
> *While he ate, the sun set beyond a dip in the rim of the curved wall. As the morning sun burst wondrously through a grand arch into this valley, in a golden, slanting shaft, so the evening sun, at the moment of setting, shone through a gap of cliffs, sending down a broad red burst to brighten the oval with a blaze of fire. To Venters, both sunrise and sunset were unreal.*[27]

For Grey, every experience with nature led to a sharpening of his art. In this sense, Grey departs from other romantic writers in that he places accurate observation on par with his action scenes. This is generally considered the domain of the realist writer. It had long been thought that the romanticist was more interested in imaginative settings than visually accurate ones, and such a tradition has produced writers like Edgar Allan Poe, Robert Louis Stevenson, Arthur Conan Doyle, and Edgar Rice Burroughs. And so this attitude—the willingness to express his atmosphere in concrete, objective terms—is what has made Grey such a memorable writer of Westerns.

His knowledge of landscape is matched by his ability to go inward and dwell in the often windy spaces and dark waters of life. Grey was not a worldly, intellectual writer in the sense of Henry James or Booth Tarkington, but the currents of his life ran deep. He was above all an emotional author. His nerve endings were particularly sensitive to people of all sorts. He liked women, for they gave him admiration and comfort. He found that he could talk to women in both an emotional and intellectual way without appearing weak. As much as women confounded him with their ways regarding romance and love, they also nurtured him with their girlish pouts, harmless flirtations, intuitive insights, and barbed opinions. He described this fascination in his diary: "I like to climb the mountains with a girl, and picture her on mossy stones, or lichen-covered cliffs, or rugged trunk or twisted pine or oak. I talk a little and listen much and feel greatly. . . . I feel all the phases of the sex sense in man. I love youth and beauty . . . the waving of hair, the action, the reality, the charm—these I feel with all the power there is in me. . . . The wonder of it all will never cease to hold me. . . . But hours with a woman on a mountain top are rich with the secrets of human life. Every step, every word, every glance has its story . . . But the flame gathering in the eye and the fire shooting through the clasped hands—these are not new to a woman. . . ."[28]

In his sequel to *Riders of the Purple Sage*, Grey rearranges the geography of northern Arizona and southern Utah to suit his storyline. For instance, *Riders* is set in and around Kanab, Utah, and spreads to Tsegi Canyon in northern Arizona. *The Rainbow Trail* was conceived through different geographical locations. Roughly speaking, the story begins in Kayenta, moves north to the Utah border and the "village of sealed wives." After Shefford and Fay escape, the narrative shifts due west to the Rainbow Bridge. Surprise Valley in *The Rainbow Trail* is actually in a different location than Tsegi Canyon, Arizona. Grey calls the entrance to it Nonnezoshe Boco, which is just east of the famous bridge. Readers are often confused by the change in locations.

Grey never meant for *The Rainbow Trail* to overshadow *Riders of the Purple Sage*. The latter is a better novel for two reasons. First, Grey created *Riders* with a string of interesting complications that needed

The walls of Marble Canyon loom over the Colorado River. Here the characters of *The Rainbow Trail* endeavored to make their escape.

ALAN LESTORGEON @SHUTTERSTOCK.COM

plausible resolutions. Second, the characters are more dynamic. Jane Withersteen and Jim Lassiter are sharply drawn, fairly nuanced characters with strong ties to the land. They are worth knowing and approachable. Jane, in particular, is the embodiment of courage and endurance. She exceeds readers' expectations of what a great heroine should be and therefore becomes a memorable character. Grey endows her with noble qualities that differentiate her from other members of her gender. Every great character of fiction must have this intimate combination of typical and individual traits. It is through being typical that her character is true. It is through being individual that her character is convincing.[29]

Some readers of *Riders* might conclude that the ending is an escape from a threatening world; others might see Jane and Lassiter's sojourn in Surprise Valley as an imprisonment. If the latter is true, then *The Rainbow Trail* is its epilogue. For some reason, perhaps obvious, readers do not want their characters to remain in paradise, if that paradise prevents them from living in a world full of people. Lassiter, Jane, and Fay are at last free, even if that liberation induces yet another series of calamities, trials, and obstacles.

CHAPTER NINE

Silent *Riders*

His name may mean nothing, but the face and the hand holding a gun mean everything.

While filming *The Great Train Robbery* in 1903, director Edwin Porter had a brilliant idea. He would dress up one of his actors in cowboy gear and have him shoot directly at the camera. Thus, Justus Barnes, clad in shirt, bandanna, and a hat shoved back to his hairline and revealing a lock of stiff hair, stood in front of the cameraman. From a distance of about three feet, he fired six shots at the viewer. After emptying the gun, he kept on pulling the trigger a few times. The scene could have been placed at the beginning or end of the movie, but Porter chose the latter.

Although it had little to do with the storyline, the ten-second sequence became famous—at times more memorable than the film itself. Justus Barnes went on to make other silent films, but then faded from sight. The shooting scene became a new way of seeing the West. Seldom if ever had a close-up brought home the real West with all its raw vigor and random violence. It was the first instance in filmmaking of introducing a distinct connection between the characters and the audience. As the years passed, it would inspire the productions of more Western films and take them from the shadows of American life into the spotlight.

This ten-minute-long, fourteen-scene movie became a milestone of early moviemaking and an inspiration to a group of Western writers, including Zane Grey. Porter introduced many new techniques in the film, but Barnes's scene captured the essence of the director's intent. The film was shot near Fort Lee, New Jersey, and lacked any real scenes of the Western landscape. Barnes's gunplay thus might have been the most authentic part of the movie. Other movies of the period, although filmed in America, depicted exotic locales such as New York, Paris, and London, but the Western gradually became as popular as the more contemporary melodramas.

By the end of 1910, when Zane Grey had received some level of notoriety with his first Western novel, several film entrepreneurs had landed in Southern California. Early pioneers in film direction, like D. W. Griffith, found that California outshone most other locations due to its climate, rugged scenery, and ocean views. They settled on a dusty strip of land located amid barley fields and occasional tumbleweed, just north of Los Angeles. Hollywood soon bustled with producers, directors, and actors who were part of a continuous invasion for the next few decades. Canadians, Britons, and Americans mingled freely, hoping to turn their talents and energies into seventeen- to twenty-minute one-reel films. Griffith soon directed *In Old California*, the first film shot in Hollywood.

In 1911 Jesse Lasky, who along with Samuel Goldwyn would go on to pioneer Paramount Pictures, acquired the rights to a popular 1905 stage play, *The Squaw Man*. Lasky believed the theater hit would transfer well to the screen. Production was scheduled to begin filming in New Jersey, but inclement weather forced alternative plans. Lasky then chose Flagstaff, due to its mountainous backdrop and ponderosa-covered hillsides. Flagstaff was still a frontier town, with one boot in the past and the other pointing to LA. As it turned out, an April snowstorm greeted the producer with five inches of snow, so Lasky kept heading west, toward Southern California. Promoted as a film "staged in the exact locale of the play," *The Squaw Man*, with a running time of seventy-two minutes, became the first feature-length movie to be filmed in California and made a star out of its lead actor, Dustin Farnum. Dustin and his younger brother, William, went on to star in several feature-length silent films.

Between 1910 and 1915, motion picture production went into overdrive. Film scripts became more complex and sophisticated; running times increased; actors and actresses, such Charlie Chaplin and Mary Pickford, entered the national consciousness. In February 1915, William Fox founded the Fox Film Corporation in Fort Lee, New Jersey. Built on a shoestring, Fox's enterprise rose swiftly, and the Hungarian-born entre-preneur eyed moving his production business to the West Coast. Like many film producers of the time, Fox stayed current on authors, both up-and-coming and established ones, especially those who had breakthrough novels and those who entered the top ten best-seller lists. Zane Grey soon began to draw his interest.

But the Harper and Brothers celebrity author and occasional husband had no business sense whatsoever. Besides attracting the attention of Fox, Grey was receiving offers from other film companies. He hired Bob Davis of *Munsey's* to broker his novels for interested movie corporations. After a few bad misfires on Grey's part, Davis told him bluntly: "Forgive me everything I have ever said to you—with the provision that I am permit-ted to reiterate the simple, unvarnished statement that you are a damned bad business man. . . . The position you occupy in American fiction is a high one and you have earned it by sheer ability, plus courage. I still insist that if I could handle you for the next five years, the Grey family would have a winter and a summer home . . . a retinue of servants, automobiles, boats, and flying machines. You never should be permitted to talk to any-body on a business proposition."[1] Davis's salvo was hardly news to Zane or Dolly. Zane had little if any interest in negotiating contracts, so he let Davis handle his business affairs with film studios.

In early 1916, William Fox approached Davis about buying the rights to *Riders of the Purple Sage*. Grey initially refused Fox's offer of $2,500 for the rights to the author's 1912 novel, but finally gave in when the movie mogul added $2,500 for *The Rainbow Trail*. Grey signed with Fox Film Corporation in March. In addition to these two Grey novels, Fox eventu-ally bought the rights to *The Lone Star Ranger*, *Last of the Duanes*, and *The Last Trail*, which left an opening for Paramount Pictures and Jesse Lasky to purchase several other Grey novels for the screen.

* * *

Sixteen years into the new century, Zane Grey was setting all sorts of sales records at Harper, but the label of "phenom" was not yet applied to him. Five years later it was. Many observers in book publishing, perhaps envi-ous of Grey's success, questioned the literary merit of his work. A large receptive audience does not necessarily indicate a great writer, but it also does not dismiss him as an inferior one.

But Grey was not without his competitors in the market. In Europe, for instance, the publishing world was still dominated by German writers like Karl May (1842–1912), who, with little training but an avid interest in the American West, turned his talent into nearly forty novels with Western themes. May was influenced by the tales of James Fenimore Cooper and he began spinning tales of the West while Zane Grey was growing up in Ohio. May created the characters of Old Shatterhand and his Indian partner, Winnetou. Although May did not visit the West until shortly before his death, he managed to invent vivid characters who captured the attention of the German reading public. So extensive was his influence that, by the turn of the twentieth century, his name was often more recognized than Goethe or Schiller.

May had a profound influence on young, impressionable men in Germany, including a budding artist by the name of Adolf Hitler. As it turned out, Hitler came to admire the lore of the West with its enduring heroes and frontier justice. When World War I broke out, the young Hitler eagerly joined a Bavarian regiment and was deployed to the front as a dispatch runner in Belgium and France. He brought along a copy of a Karl May novel. Perhaps it's not too much of a stretch to imagine the young Austrian corporal reading May in his leisure time in a trench while across the barbed wire a British Tommy or American doughboy was deep in *Riders of the Purple Sage* or *Desert Gold.* There have been many reasons advanced for Hitler's attraction to Westerns, but perhaps the simplest one was that he liked their brave *Kavaliere*, frontier drama, and quick justice. He used such aspects to master and eventually enslave a nation. When Hitler's personal architect, Albert Speer, surrendered in 1945, he muttered, "So now the end has come. That's good. It was all only a kind of opera anyway."

Closer to home, Friedrich Schiller Faust, better known by his pen name of Max Brand, began his writing career during the Great War. After graduating from the University of California at Berkeley, Brand tried to work his way out of Grubstreet by writing magazine articles. One of Brand's first contacts in New York was Grey's film agent, Bob Davis of *Munsey's*. Davis stared at the newcomer. "You're supposed to be able to write," snapped Davis, handing him a sheet of paper. "Here's a plot. There's an empty room down the hall with a typewriter and a ream of paper in it. Go down there, if you like, and see if you can write a story. Third door on the right."

Brand did as he was told, banging away at the typewriter in the little room down the hall. Nearly seven hours later, Brand brought Davis a freshly typed manuscript of about one hundred pages. Amazed by Faust's accomplishment, Davis glanced over the writer's fine work.

"Where did you learn to write like that?" asked Davis.

Brand said, "Third door on the right, down the hall."[2]

Max Brand quickly rose in the field of Western writing. Although he cared little for the lore of the West, once calling it "disgusting," he managed to write several strong titles featuring the West and mined its endless resources for fiction. Intent on capturing the timelessness of classical literature, Brand created Western heroes from his imagination, learning writing tips along the way from Grey and other authors. Davis started Brand writing for one of his magazines, *All Star Weekly*. In late 1918 the magazine featured Brand's first Western, *The Untamed*, which introduced the lead character Whistling Dan Barry.

The novel became so successful that it launched Brand's career, which prompted many observers to claim that "another Zane Grey" had indeed been found. Brand wrote other classics in the genre, including *Destry Rides Again* (1930) and *The Iron Trail* (1938). He also wrote under seventeen different pen names in genres ranging from the Western to detective and war stories. Although his output was prodigious over the course of his career, he groaned under the weight of his writing empire. "Daily," Brand admitted, "I thank God in three languages that I write under a pen name."[3]

Had Max Brand begun his career ten years earlier, say, in 1909, he could have been a major threat to Zane Grey. But as it was, Grey had just the right timing to spark the Western and to take advantage of the booming film industry. Plus, Grey had rawness to his prose and a love of the West, qualities that Brand lacked. Over time, these features became apparent to Grey's readers, and they helped his books to endure the years with their authenticity.

* * *

Despite all of the drawbacks of silent movies—lack of sound, poor quality film, and primitive cameras—audiences flocked to them. It was naturally assumed by many people that film pioneers had extensive backgrounds in the movie industry. But most film moguls had no formal training in movie production. Griffith worked in a dry goods store as a teenager. Goldwyn was born in Poland, struggled with poverty, and had trained as a glove maker. Fox was born in Hungary and schooled in the garment industry. All three rose as apprentices, learning what they could by being totally dedicated to their craft.

Hollywood produced every type of motion picture that sold. Romantic comedies, screwball humoresques, horror flicks, costume melodramas, literary classics, and historical melodramas could be filmed on makeshift Hollywood sets or nearby in the Hollywood hills. Sets were often erected overnight, using whatever cheap material was close at hand—plywood or even cardboard fastened with two-by-fours or nailed with carpet tacks. Westerns, however, soon demanded greater space and more scenic backdrops. When Grey signed with Fox Film Corporation, he stipulated that he wished to be consulted on all location shoots to ensure that they were as close as possible to the locales mentioned in his novels. In some cases, such as with *Riders of the Purple Sage* and *The Rainbow Trail*, both filmed in 1918, this was not an issue. Northern Arizona was near enough to Los Angeles to facilitate transporting a film crew. Grey was insistent that the action not be filmed on a Hollywood back lot or in the San Fernando Valley, which had dusty trails and rocks but not the atmosphere Grey demanded.

Consequently, the filming of *Riders* required an army of production staff to load their equipment on an eastbound train heading for Flagstaff. Horses, wagons, and any additional props were requisitioned from the ranches near the location shoot. With each new Western, directors insisted locations have more space and scenic backgrounds. Directors insisted on enough level terrain to film stampedes, runaway stagecoaches, horse chases, and fistfights. The foregrounds and backgrounds of Westerns were as carefully chosen as the actors and actresses. Since color was not an issue, directors highlighted the size and unique shapes of mesas, buttes, crags, and mountains.

Due to the limited number of takes and the short running time of movies (between sixty and seventy-five minutes), directors could make multiple films in one calendar year. Frank Lloyd, who directed the first *Riders of the Purple Sage*, supervised twelve films in 1916. Similarly, writers could tackle twenty to twenty-five films a year. But, as sound movies transitioned in, directors slowed their pace to four to five films a year; writers followed suit.

The advent of the silent film era opened significant opportunities for new writers. Southern California was home to a hotbed of talented screenwriters, some of whom were refugees from New York fleeing the saturation of magazines and newspapers. Among this group was a thirty-something native of Minnesota named C. Gardiner Sullivan, who arrived in Hollywood after spending a few years at the *New York Evening Journal*. In Hollywood, he began writing titles for one-reel films, then progressed into two-reelers, and, finally in 1915, began writing feature scenarios for the films of William S. Hart, the screen's biggest Western star.

In 1916, Sullivan handed his script for *Hell's Hinges* to Hart and director Charles Swickard (who later would direct Grey's *The Light of Western Stars*). The steely eyed and razor-jawed Hart turned a yarn with a simple plot into a revolutionary Western. *Hell's Hinges* lifted the genre from a humdrum melodrama into a serious study of crime and revenge. Many called it Hart's masterpiece. The *New York Press* observed that "gunplay and religion lubricate *Hell's Hinges*" and declared that William S. Hart was an absolute original. "No actor before the screen," the review continued, "has been able to give as sincere and true a touch to a Westerner as Hart. He rides in a manner indigenous to the soil. He shoots with the real knack, and he acts with that sense of artistry that hides the acting."[4]

Hell's Hinges set the standard for the Western for the next several years. Fox and Paramount studio bosses directed their production staffs to study the techniques used in the film to shape some of their Western scenes.

* * *

In April 1918, production of the first *Riders of the Purple Sage* for the screen was set and ready to begin filming in the Painted Desert of Arizona. Frank Lloyd, the director and writer, had spent the previous winter reading Grey's novel and composing the scenario for the movie. Lloyd was British born and learned the art of direction by first acting in several low-budget two-reel Westerns. He cowrote *The Rainbow Trail* with Charles Kenyon. Both films were included as a package for filming, since *The Rainbow Trail* continued the storyline of *Riders*. Fox and Lloyd had no issue with the Mormon angle, so the director followed Grey's narrative faithfully. Not all novels are constructed so that they translate well to the stage or the screen, but *Riders of the Purple Sage*, with its dramatic scenes featuring Venters and Tull, Lassiter and Dyer, Jane and her congregation, made the transition relatively easy for Lloyd.

The cast included William Farnum as Lassiter and Mary Mersch as Jane. Farnum was a veteran screen actor and had become nearly as famous as William Hart in heroic roles. He made his screen debut in Rex Beach's *The Spoilers* (1914). He and his brother Dustin were among the most highly regarded screen actors of the second decade of the century. But he was no William S. Hart. For one thing, he did not have Hart's authenticty of character.

At the time of filming, Farnum was a tad paunchy and did not look the part of a gunman who had ambled along through the canyons and gulches of the region. He had a shock of hair that frizzed in humid air and went straight in the dry air of Arizona. As Lassiter, he wore black from head to foot. He wore his gun belt slung low. He could look fierce on cue, particularly when defending Jane, and then melt into her arms in the next scene. His speaking voice was raspy and muddled, but since it didn't matter on screen, his facial expressions carried him through the various scenes. Farnum was durable and steady, although he did not measure up to the stature of the Lassiter character in the novel.

Mersch was cast in her first starring role as Jane Withersteen, having played supporting characters in twelve previous films. Veteran heavies Murdock MacQuarrie and Marc Robbins donned long dark coats as the nefarious Elder Tull and Bishop Dyer, respectively; rounding out the

Often visiting the filming sites of his novels, Zane Grey here poses in front of the Western set for 1918's *Riders of the Purple Sage.*

cast were William Scott as Venters, Nancy Caswell as Fay, and Kathryn Adams as Millie.

Frank Lloyd had little experience in location shooting and the vast Arizona canvas gave him something of a challenge. Organizing all the features of a Western intimidated him, so that his camera angles were not creative enough for this large-scale operation. At times, he did not get enough from his leading actors in particular scenes, so this tended to limit the power of the film. But the first filming of *Riders of the Purple Sage*, on balance, was a success. The northern Arizona backdrops helped lift an otherwise standard movie into one of the best Westerns of the second decade of the century.

Due to the limitations of the camera lenses, directors could not take great advantage of the stunning backdrops that characterized many of John Ford's films in later decades. Monument Valley was not yet a treasured location for filming. Until better lenses were perfected, the camera failed to capture the magisterial quality of Southwestern landmarks. On film they always appeared a great distance away, despite how they looked in reality. In these years, the emphasis was on the characters and their actions. Romantic scenes and gunfights were favored over scenic backdrops. In this sense, the desert, pillars, and canyons were not characters in themselves.

The Rainbow Trail, filmed on the heels of *Riders*, with William Foster behind the camera, was shot near Page, Arizona, which stood in admirably for the escape scenes around the Rainbow Bridge. Foster framed some brilliant shots of Shefford, Nas ta Bega, and Fay as they toiled their way to Surprise Valley. William Farnum and Mary Mersch reprised their roles from *Riders of the Purple Sage*. Farnum played both Shefford and Lassiter, while Ann Forest portrayed a mature Fay Larkin. William Burress was cast as the surly Waggoner. Probably the one good thing to come out of the film was that Lloyd refused to cast Lassiter as a stumbling old man, but simply added twelve years to the character by applying some pancake makeup to Farnum and streaking gray through his hair.

Grey visited the set during filming and had the crew take his picture on horseback wearing a wool shirt, a bandana, chaps, and a cowboy hat. At forty-six years of age, he was still a boy in dungarees. The process of

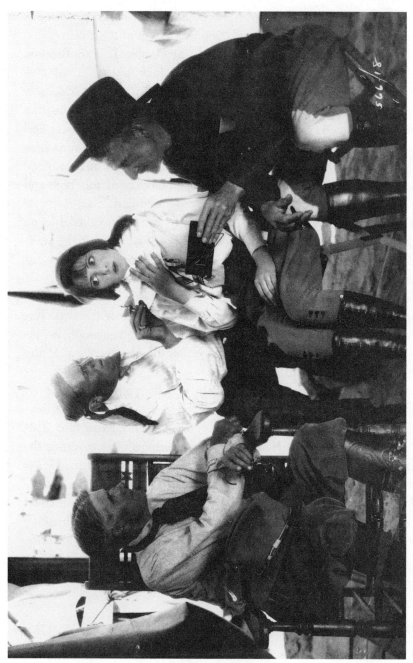

Zane Grey (left) joins actress Billie Dove and crewmembers on the set of *Wild Horse Mesa* (1925).

filmmaking always fascinated Grey, and eventually he began to write his articles based on some of the crosscutting techniques of the cinema.

Riders of the Purple Sage was released on September 1, 1918. Reviews were generally positive, but *Variety* observed that it was "a not-too-absorbing adaptation of the novel by Zane Grey. The story is told loosely with much riding hither and yon, and finally comes to a halt with the expenditure of much energy on the part of the actors and not a great deal of interest on the part of the spectator. Mr. Farnum makes a stalwart Lassiter, doing well when he is called upon to do so. The picture does not rise above the level of the average Western photoplay of this type and there is no special distinction in direction or photography."[5] *The Rainbow Trail* debuted on October 27, 1918. *Motion Picture News* called Lloyd's film "a fair Western with lots of rough stuff and should pass if the audiences like William Farnum's work."[6] Unfortunately, both films are missing, presumed lost.

Reviews of new films were typically done by *Variety*, established in 1905, and *Motion Picture News*, begun in 1913. Most of the reviewers lacked training or skill in the art of criticism. They were generally beginning writers who did their best to say something serious about a film but ended up writing fluff and nonsense. At first, only a few films per year were reviewed. Between March 1911 and December 1912, *Variety* even discontinued reviews because it believed that advertising a particular film brought an unfair advantage to certain studios. Most film criticism was done anonymously, an indication, perhaps, that covering the motion picture industry was a sideline occupation for journalists. *Variety* often encouraged film critics to use four-letter pen names such as "Rush," "Bell," or "Herm" to identify their copy. Reviewers were mainly focused on the star aspect of films, and the more consequential parts of filmmaking eluded them. It wasn't until the 1930s and 40s that valuable movie criticism entered the mainstream and became as important as book and art reviews in newspapers and journals.

* * *

Despite his successes in film and book publishing with Harper, Grey struggled with bipolar disorder, exacerbated by the Great War in Europe and his relationship with Dolly. The war affected Grey deeply. He wrote in his diary: "This war has upset my mental equilibrium. It's a bad time for thinking men and fatal for an idealist."[7] The great optimism that characterized the beginning years of the century was sinking into the mud of France. "Where was the glory and dream?" he wondered. The milk of human kindness had seemingly evaporated. He was a hollow man. "Last night while I was awake, though lying with closed eyes, I thought of myself in this way. I can bear defeat, but not loss of all, not at one fell swoop. Loss of family, friends, loss of power to write! Loss of virility, strength, eyesight! What horror! I conquer one mood only to fall prey to the next."[8] His wife reminded him that he must exercise more, which he did. But despite all his attempts at exercise, fishing, friendships, marriage, fatherhood, and traveling, he knew that writing was his last salvation.

He and Dolly vacillated between love and resentment. Zane spent most of the winter months in Long Key, Florida, or on Catalina Island. His angling records were mounting. He traveled when needed to New York or the Southwest, or when the spirit called, to almost anywhere. Dolly's younger cousins often accompanied him. Their relationship to Grey was somewhat amorphous. What exactly was their connection to Zane? The answer perplexed even Dolly, who appeared to be sufficiently passive enough to let the practice continue. Were they girlfriends, traveling companions, protégés, secretaries, gold diggers, or what? To compound matters, Zane was never sure himself.

If they weren't at sword's point at home, the spouses dueled from afar. Grey wrote Dolly: "My friends are not what you think them. They all have weaknesses, as indeed the whole race has, but they are worth to me all and more than I have given them. . . . These girls have kept something vital alive in me."[9]

The "girls" Grey referred to included Lillian Wilhelm; Lillian's younger sister, Claire; and Elma Swartz, Mildred Smith, and Dorothy Ackerman. These relationships were not totally out of bounds in the current culture of America, but Dolly grudgingly tolerated Grey's apparent need for admiration and encouragement from these women. In one letter Grey complained that Catalina Island offered little in the way of entertainment. Baring her claws, Dolly sarcastically replied: "How can you be as supremely egotistical and selfish as to drag your tender young friends and sensitive relatives to a 'hole' like Catalina? No place to eat, no nice accommodations, not one damned thing to do . . . your letter was a masterpiece. It should be published from an altruistic point of view. Think of all the wives left home who would be infinitely comforted and uplifted by its contents."[10]

Crushed by her response, he could easily drift into self-pity and playing the victim: "You make me see," he wrote back, "that I am only a dog, a cur, when I could go on dreaming if my frailties were not so pointed out. You have made me lose faith in myself. I think I might have made some kind of a real success in life if I had been allowed to go on in my own way."[11]

These letters back and forth are filled with morbid teasing; at times, they could be much lighter in tone, but the underlying message was the same: come home and be the husband you pretend to be. Zane, of course, was lucky to have such an understanding spouse as Dolly. Some husbands of the era who behaved like Grey would find their fishing tackle, wading boots, and belongings scattered on the front lawn.

Many people close to the Greys might have wondered why they engaged in so much drama and turmoil. Why not get a divorce and remove all the bitterness and agony? It was a good question, but only Zane and Dolly could answer it. However, they were too involved in moving to Los Angeles, where they both planned on patching up their marriage and beginning a new life.

Zane had been scouting suitable areas in Los Angeles throughout 1918. The demands of the film industry coupled with his love for deep-sea fishing affected his decision to move to Southern California permanently. The train journey from New York to Los Angeles took four to five days one way. Moreover, he was nearing his fiftieth birthday, and it seemed like a good time to be acting like it.

He could at write two good-size novels in a year, but Duneka wanted to release only one a year. Harper's reasoning paid off, for the wait between books made sales soar upon publication. Grey began to stockpile novels, so that he could be well ahead of a book's release schedule. *The U.P. Trail* shot to the top of the best-seller lists for 1918 and helped him become one of the five wealthiest authors in America.

Zane loved the outdoors and enjoyed nature all around him.

In the early months of 1919, Grey headed to Death Valley, where he began work on what he considered his most important novel. For several days Zane and his companion Sievert Nielsen probed the silent wastes of one of the hottest and deadliest places on earth. He had chosen this desolate region as the setting for *Wanderer of the Wasteland* (1923), the book that he believed would make him not only a best-selling novelist but also one of literary distinction. By completing his trek through Death Valley, he was really trying to resolve some inner struggle and to understand the depths of his own isolation.

If *Riders of the Purple Sage* is Grey's best novel, then *Wanderer of the Wasteland* is a close second. *Wanderer* is an enigmatic novel and one that would have a passionate, writhing birth. Grey realized that before beginning any novel he had moments of absolute despair and fear of "the white bull."

"This novel," he remarked, "will not be great unless I have absolute control and restraint. I am absolutely determined that it will be a great novel. I must look out for nervous strain. I must not hurry. I must not try to do too much in a short time . . . I must be prepared to expect depressions and to understand them, and to meet them with intelligence and counteraction, with change and will." A month into the writing of the novel, Zane noted: "I shall take time with this great book. It grows and grows . . . I shall utterly spend myself, my passion and soul on it before I finish." Four days later, on January 13, he confessed: "Today I am sore, angry, bitter, hopeless . . . the mood lingers. I had the most trying time, sitting here making scratches on my manuscript."[12]

In May of 1919 Grey completed his novel—838 handwritten pages, one hundred and seventy thousand words. At midnight toward the end of the month, he jotted in his diary: "I have just ended my novel *Wanderer of the Wasteland* . . . and I sweat blood."[13]

Zane had begun his novel barely a month and half after the end of the World War. The novel's setting may be the California desert, but there is an additional theme in the book. After the war, a period of sadness and disillusionment settled on the country and the world. People were shocked by the brutality and carnage of the conflict. Writers and artists, in particular, were affected by the hollowness of life. Grey, too, felt an emptiness that he could not explain. The opening decade of the century had begun with such buoyant optimism, only to be shattered by four long years of death and destruction. Consequently, *Wanderer of the Wasteland* offers the reader a glimpse of another side of Zane Grey, one that features a counterpoint to his earlier romance novels such as *Riders of the Purple Sage*, *The Rainbow Trail*, *The Light of Western Stars*, and *Desert Gold*.

Grey turned to writing to overcome his disenchantment with the postwar period; others, of course, turned to different behaviors, some beneficial, some dangerous, but anything to bandage the wound.

* * *

The literary critics, mostly from eastern newspapers and journals, generally disliked Zane Grey's work. By 1920 his novels, in their opinion, had become formulaic, sentimental, and predictable. Two of the most vocal critics on the literary and theater scene were Burton Rascoe and Heywood Broun. Both were beginning their careers in large newspapers with wide readerships and were eager to make their marks. Rascoe was a University of Chicago-trained journalist who leaned toward the realist school of writing; Broun was known for his rumpled appearance, which prompted one observer to remark that he looked like "an unmade bed." Broun, too, favored realism in the arts.

They were not alone. Mark Twain's observation that the school of romanticism was a "dead letter" was in the mainstream of American criticism. Grey's brand of Western romance was decidedly out of favor among the literary elite. Moreover, writers who perennially made the top ten best-seller lists were suspect, and critics zeroed in on their success. Rascoe called Grey's "moral ideas decidedly askew. Do [readers] accept the code of conduct implicit in Grey's novels?" Rascoe was referring to characters in Grey's novels who meddle in other people's lives and influence their decision-making. In another newspaper's review, Broun remarked that "all of Grey's work could be written on the back of a postage stamp," summing up the general feeling toward the popular Western. At the time, it was not customary to review Westerns as part of a genre, that is, to compare Westerns with Westerns, mysteries with mysteries, and so on. As a result, Grey had to compete with a diverse collection of novels at any given time.

Although Grey had a vast number of eager fans, he yearned for critical acceptance: "Sometimes when I read a splendid review of a book I am at once uplifted and then cast down. I have never gotten the kind of criticism that I yearn for. My books do not receive serious reviews. Not one of those higher classes of critics takes me seriously, if he ever reads me at all. I confess to a suspicion that my books are not read by the critical elect. Always this indifference to my efforts, to what I have tried to do, if not the result, has hurt me. . . . Someday I shall drive past this barren cold coterie of arbiters."[14]

Grey wearied of critics and readers who didn't know what they were talking about. After seething about it for several years, in the early 1920s he sat down and wrote "My Answer to the Critics." It was a twenty-page rant about how critics understood very little about the West. He said that from the beginning he wished to "reach a great audience. I chose to win that [audience] through romance, adventure, and love of the wild and beautiful nature. The West appealed tremendously to my imagination. I hoped that critics would judge me not from the result but from the nature of my effort." Grey also tried to defend his approach to Western themes and characters by claiming that he had known many men like Bern Venters in *Riders of the Purple Sage* and met women as "sweet and ignorant of life as Fay Larkin in *The Rainbow Trail*." Grey continued by saying that "Western people know that I am absolutely true to the settings of my romances." He directed the critics to ask the people who read his books—the janitor, the plumber, the fireman, and the engineer. These are the readers, Grey claimed, who should be commenting objectively on his novels. The critics "do not know."[15]

As an early fabulist, Grey wanted to be considered much more than just a second-generation dime novelist. He wished to be an authentic Westerner, writing vivid stories of the pioneers who encountered the labors and dangers of the frontier. Although his characters and settings changed, his narrative voice remained consistent. It was a voice that readers of Zane Grey could easily recognize. He wrote in strong, tight sentences, packed with local color. In real life, he was always a man of action. In his fishing articles and his Western novels, he propelled the story forward at a brisk pace. He was restless, moody, exuberant, and impulsive; his body was always in motion. Likewise, his stories moved quickly forward to some fulfilling resolution.

Critics of the time considered Grey's prodigious output—one novel a year, plus one in readiness—a sign he was only seeking commercial success. They looked for some literary quality in each new book. The fact remained that Grey was the only Western writer perennially on the best-seller list between 1914 and 1930. "They do not know" remained his mantra.

Grey, Brand, and later Ernest Haycox, Will Henry, Luke Short, and Louis L'Amour promoted a concept of the West that was more fantasy than reality, and this concept was always in conflict with another group of writers who wished to represent the complexity and drama of human existence in a Western setting. The terms "Western Novel" and "A Novel of the West" have come to be used as a way of distinguishing the former from the latter. Down the road for Grey and his followers were such developments as sound movies and the paperback book, both of which energized the Western as a truly American art form.

The need for Grey to respond to critics quickly faded, as he went on to other novels, other angling waters, other women.

Toward the end of 1923, William Fox called and told him the studio was planning a remake of *Riders of the Purple Sage*. Filming would begin the following year. Would he be available to advise on some casting decisions?

* * *

In the seven-year span between the first *Riders* of William Farnum and the 1925 remake starring Tom Mix, the motion picture industry had made leaps forward in film quality, direction, and acting. The number of Westerns being produced had doubled. Directed by John Ford, *The Iron Horse* of 1924, which featured future Zane Grey star George O'Brien, became one of the most influential Western films of the decade.

Perhaps the one great feature of silent film Westerns was that they created images that haunted the imagination. Before actors started talking in film, the landscape had to serve a major purpose. Each frame, each sequence had to fit in the mind of the viewer for the storyline to be compelling. Most directors of Westerns of the time emphasized the story and action, but film pioneers like thirty-year-old John Ford realized those aspects alone do not make a great motion picture.

After making thirty-six movies for Universal Studios, Ford moved to Fox in 1920 and began making serious films, usually Westerns, for the screen. He and William Fox had a tense relationship. The studio mogul, known for round-the-clock supervision of his production company, demanded directors check in with him, remain under budget, and stay on time. John Ford, however, started mounting large-scale operations on locations that went over budget and exceeded Fox's time frame for shooting.

On location for *The Iron Horse* in the Sierra Nevada near Lone Pine, California, Ford amassed an army for his film about the completion of the transcontinental railroad in 1869. The studio gave Ford a $280,000 budget to work within and a shooting schedule of four months. Ford's silent epic used five thousand extras (including a detachment of cavalry), two thousand rail layers, eight hundred Indians, two thousand horses, ten thousand head of cattle, and thirteen hundred buffaloes. The Western had moved into the era of bigger is better.

Filming fell behind schedule and Ford began to blow the lid off his budget. Frustrated by repeated delays in filming, studio executives fired off telegrams to Ford, demanding that he explain his reasons for tying up money and time. When Ford received the telegrams, he reportedly tore them up or had his stuntman, Ed "Pardner" Jones, use them for target practice. Eventually, Ford's artful direction of *The Iron Horse* paid off, raking in an estimated $2 million at the box office.

William Fox eyed Lynn Reynolds to helm *Riders of the Purple Sage*. Reynolds, who had worked with William Farnum and Tom Mix in earlier films, was the logical choice due to his friendship and working relationship with Mix. In 1924 Tom Mix got the role of Jim Lassiter and further established his superstar status. Screen veteran Mabel Ballin was cast as Jane Withersteen. Ballin, at thirty-seven years old, was considered one of the most beautiful women in Hollywood.

Film studios rarely invite the author of a novel to also write the screenplay, and Grey probably would have refused William Fox anyway, simply believing that he had no talent for such a project. Instead, Fox brought in Edfrid Bingham to write the script for the 1925 version of

Lone Pine, California, provided the dramatic backdrop for Mix's action scenes in Fox Film's 1925 adaptation of *Riders*.
KEN KISTLER @SHUTTERSTOCK.COM

Riders. He had previously served as head screenwriter for Grey's *Call of the Canyon* (1923), which was filmed in Sedona. With its dense foregrounds of piñon and juniper, its magisterial, red-tinged rock formations and receding vistas, Sedona became a prime shooting location, largely because of the success of *Call of the Canyon*.

Grey wanted to film *Riders* in Sedona, but Fox and Reynolds had already chosen Lone Pine because it offered greater space for the movement of horses, actors, and film crews. Largely due to its carpets of purple sage in the foreground, rocky foothills, and the lofty Sierras in the distance, Lone Pine proved a worthy substitute for southern Utah. It also boasted some of the most distinctive rock formations on the continent—not necessarily as colorful as in Arizona, but unique nonetheless. Production started a short time after Ford's *The Iron Trail* had finished decamping and left the area.

If fans didn't know Tom Mix before he posed—proudly and often—in his immaculate, white ten-gallon hat for the press, they never failed to recognize him in movie after movie, tearing across the rugged chaparral on his noble steed, Tony. Grey did not choose Mix for the lead role; that honor went to Fox and Reynolds. Zane consented to the casting, knowing that Mix would give the film some instant notoriety.

Like many leading actors and notable directors of the silent film era, Mix held a variety of odd jobs early in his career. Born in Pennsylvania in 1880, Mix worked as a bartender, roustabout, and ranch foreman before joining a touring Wild West show that gave performances in Colorado and Prescott, Arizona. He was always a skilled horseman and generally performed his own stunts in the many one- and two-reelers of the early years of film. He was perhaps the most famous rider of the silent film era. Along with later motion picture stunt riders, such as Yakima Canutt and Ben Johnson, he made the Western—well, move. John Ford, in particular, favored authentic riders in his films. In *Stagecoach* (with Canutt), *Fort Apache*, *She Wore a Yellow Ribbon*, *Rio Grande*, and *Wagon Master* (with Johnson), the accomplished movie horseman came into his own.

Academy Award winner Ben Johnson had it all—looks, charisma, extraordinary riding skill, daring, and a humility that filled the screen. John Wayne, who starred with Johnson in several Ford films, may have been a screen cowboy, but Johnson was the genuine article. Because of his convincing Western aura, Johnson was one the few supporting actors who could make Wayne soften into butter.

Mix may have been the most recognized movie cowboy in America, but there were roles that did not fit his cavalier spirit. Mix as Lassiter in the 1925 *Riders of the Purple Sage* was one. The part called for a rider, gunfighter, and loner, a man laconic but not timid, whose features have been chiseled away by time, weather, and disappointment.

With his casual manner, Mix may have been too breezy for the role. He was old enough to play the hero, but too often his rodeo tricks defeated the steadfast character of Lassiter. Mabel Ballin as Jane did her best to make the character a "modern woman." The athletic Harold Goodwin played Bern Venters, and legendary Gary Cooper, in one of his first but uncredited screen roles, rode in Tull's band of followers. Cooper would go on the following year to his breakout role in Henry King's *The Winning of Barbara Worth*, based on the novel by Harold Bell Wright. In 1927 Cooper starred in Grey's *Nevada*, and in 1929 in Wister's *The Virginian*.

Filmed in the panoramic Alabama Hills near Lone Pine, this remake of *Riders of the Purple Sage* holds up much better than its 1918 predecessor, largely due to Bingham's script. One of the writer's first hurdles was incorporating Lassiter's backstory and his motivations for coming to Cottonwoods. While Grey handled this smoothly in his narrative by allowing the character to relay this information as the story developed, Bingham believed this technique would not work on film, since the many intertitles needed would slow down the action. Instead, Bingham wrote the backstory at the beginning eleven minutes of the film so the events afterward fell into logical sequence.

Trading his white hat for a black one, Mix went through his paces. His riding skill was amply demonstrated throughout the film. When he handled a gun, he went into his trademark crouch position before firing. With knees braced and body crouched low, he was less of a target but was also able to steady the gun, a technique that Hollywood directors never fully understood. In a showdown between gunfighters, they tended to emphasize the speed of the draw, but the true test of a fast gun was his ability to draw and then steady the quivering gun long enough to fire an accurate shot.

The film was released on March 15, 1925, and opened to poor reviews. The *New York Times* reported: "If one were able to have a haircut and shave while viewing Tom Mix's latest picture, it would prove a far more entertaining effort than it is when sitting still twiddling one's thumbs and permitting one's mind to wander on Zane Grey's many stories of heroes, villains, and bullets."[16]

Like William Farnum in the earlier film, Mix played Shefford in *The Rainbow Trail*, which was filmed directly after *Riders* and opened on May 24, 1925. Directed and adapted for the screen by Reynolds, much of the action was filmed in northern Arizona and finished at the Fox lot in Glendale, California. The "aged" Lassiter was played by Doc Roberts, in his only credited screen role. *The Rainbow Trail* received more positive criticism than its predecessor, with *Variety* leading the praise: "A wow of an action Western that has Tom Mix doing all sorts of stunts to keep the audience on the edge of their seats. It is one of the best action Westerns even this star has turned out . . . The story is not one of the best Zane Grey has turned out, but serves its purpose in giving the king of Westerns a role that permits him to put Tony though a flock of steps for the benefit of his admirers."[17]

For many years afterward, *The Rainbow Trail* was thought to have perished in the Fox vault fire in 1937, which occurred at the storage facility in Little Ferry, New Jersey, and destroyed many of the silent films treated with flammable nitrate. Two of Mix's films, *Sky High* (1922) and *Riders of the Purple Sage* (1925), escaped the destruction and were considered the only films of Mix to do so. But in the 1960s, Twentieth Century Fox launched a program to retrieve some of its film heritage and discovered several Mix titles in their original format. Among the films was *The Rainbow Trail*, which at long last was reunited with its 1925 sibling.

* * *

For Zane Grey, the last years of the silent film era were spent far from the canyons and rain-washed skies of his beloved West. Fox and Paramount Pictures had together filmed forty-four movies based on Zane Grey stories, and several more were readied for the new sound film era.

In the late 1920s, Grey's fame and wealth had driven him to seek other horizons.

In 1924 he had purchased a reconditioned, three-masted schooner he named the *Fisherman*, which took him deep into Pacific waters, heading first to South America and then on to Tahiti. Therefore, Grey missed the heyday of Tom Mix and the rise of Gary Cooper in the films of his novels. But the Greys had seemingly become a happy if unusual couple. They believed in the division of labor: Dolly toiled at home, raising a family and editing Zane's manuscripts, while Zane labored on his schooner and found adventures in the purple ports of the South Pacific. He was, however, always busy writing a new Western romance. "Where do I find these romances? I see these romances and I believe them. Somewhere, sometime they happened," he mused.[18]

Zane and Dolly rarely saw each other during the period between 1925 and 1930. They had celebrated their twentieth wedding anniversary in November 1925. Their children were maturing and experiencing all the exhilaration and turmoil of their teen years. Excerpts from Zane and Dolly's letters to each other reveal the status of their marriage, their concern for their children, and the direction of Grey's writing career.

In a letter dated December 31, 1925, Zane writes from somewhere in the Pacific Ocean: "I have not been very well today. Just escaped cold or grippe in San Francisco. I ache all over, and feel pretty badly. . . . I smashed my right thumb in the door. It hurts dreadfully, and makes it almost impossible to write. Then I tried to make myself agreeable to a man onboard who claimed to know the Wetherills, and I had my feelings hurt for my pains. I got to spouting about big fish, and the damned fool said he wondered how so old a man as I dared to be so strenuous. He said surely I must be 60. Ye Gods! . . . I guess I'm a misfit among people. I wish to God I was back home . . . Happy New Year, my dearest wife, my anchor. I have absolute faith in your power to make it happy."

Now in New Zealand, Zane notes in a letter dated February 15, 1926: "I might die away from home. Then you would never know. It is a distressing thought. On the boat for hours out on the sea, you are in my mind, grateful, beautiful, loving remembrances. At night in the silence, or when the wind and the sea roar, I lie awake in my tent with thought no stenographer could even transcribe. I am so much away from you all and life is so short. I have done so ill with my talent! What might have been! What a name I might have made! What a home I might have fathered."

Dolly writes Zane on September 14, 1926: "I went see *Don Juan* last night. I am not prissy, but the amours of men are rather disgusting to me—they have to have them but why disclose them so deliberately on the screen? I often think [Byron's] poem influenced your life powerfully . . . I believe you have always had to live in a romance of which you were the hero . . . Your own powerful personality, your predilections worked in with these. . . . You're a great man, and you're out of it to be a fine man also, but it's rather appalling to look back."

While Zane was away, rumors of divorce continued to surface among Dolly's friends and family; parts of the gossip leaked out to Zane in the South Pacific. On January 23, 1927, Dolly writes to reassure him: "Don't worry about that silly divorce business. It's not a scandal, as you dub it. You know that divorce has never entered my mind. I can't conceive of such a thing when we love each other as we do, and always shall. And divorce would never solve any problems for you and me. . . . Why, even if we weren't bound by indissolvable ties, by the children, by your work—do you think I'd give any female the chance to get you? I'd shoot her first with buckshot."

Later in the same year, Zane received a letter from Dolly, dated April 2, 1927, in Tahiti: "My dear, I have been absolutely faithful to your commands. The manuscripts were finished and went off long ago. Your employees' wages were paid on the dot, even though I starve myself. I work till my head whirls, all to the glory and comfort of my husband! And that reminds me—do not forget your solemn promise to write nothing that I do not see before publication. I find so many things that would cause people and critics (are critics people?) to react unfavorably . . . your power has always lived in your emotion, and your ability to get it into your books and thus transmit it to your reader. . . . A book lives by its universality, its significance for life—that is, its power to uplift, to inculcate standards and ideals for many. There seems to be no doubt that you have this gift."

Zane, his son Romer, now nineteen years old, and some sailing friends pulled into Papeete, Tahiti, in mid-1928. He writes Dolly on September

11: "Romer is doing very well indeed, a great improvement over last year. Only twice has he been uppish. I seem to get along so much better with him, thanks to your advice. . . . I am ahead of my novel *The Drift Fence*, and up to date in my fishing notes. I shall do even better from now on, as I expect to get rid of the ship and a lot of this crowd. . . . Don't let the studio people put over any more jobs on me. Both "Avalanche" and *Sunset Pass* have to be made in Arizona, and with Lee Doyle handling locations. . . . If you can give me any news about my books, etc., I'd appreciate it. Not that I am discouraged at all! But I just wonder when I shall have to stop writing fast and furiously, and settle down to real serious work. Remember, Dolly, that I trust you to tell me when I should do this. I'm not afraid of my stories, but I am of the publishers, editors, and reviewers."

In Tahiti, Zane established his own fishing camp, named Flower Point Camp, located near Papeete. On September 27, 1928, he remarks to Dolly: "I finished *The Drift Fence*. 466 pages, 57 days. Never missed a day! 5am to 7am, most of the work, though I had a few stormy days. It was some stunt. If the work is good, I sure have discovered something. . . . It is glorious up here. Cool, breezy, above sea and canyon, with the mountains close, and the reef booming its grand melody. And I've had something I could eat. On the ship I ate nothing and got thin. Our stores are sadly depleted. First by theft of those on board, and then by bugs, etc. . . . Lost about all the jams, cookies, etc., things we can't buy here. I do get sore at those Bolsheviks I have to hire in the US. The natives I have are simply fine."

Because the seasons in the Southern Hemisphere are reversed, Zane planned many of his trips from September through March, which meant that he was not home for traditional holidays with Dolly and his family. In 1928, the fishing in Tahiti was poor, so he set sail for New Zealand, setting up camp at Mercury Bay on the north island.

In Altadena, Dolly prepared for the Christmas holiday season without her husband and Romer. She writes Zane on December 23, 1928: "Do you realize your daughter is talented? She has a marvelously poetic imagination and writes beautiful poetry and other things. Very high brow. They say she has a brilliant mind." Switching gears, Dolly continues: "My dear, don't ever worry about your reading audience. No magazines are going to pay $65,000 for a story from you if you are waning. I was in Bullock's book department yesterday and on all sides I heard people clamoring for Zane Grey. I'll take my oath that by and large you're the biggest seller in the world right now, despite any Bookman lists."

Despite being one of the highest-paid authors in the world, Zane lived life on the financial edge. His numerous expenses involving angling expeditions, fishing gear, employee wages—and generally his ravenous appetite for life—always exceeded his income from books, films, and investments. As the bills mounted at home, he could easily blame Dolly for spending too much money on her own desires and the needs of the children, as evidenced in a letter of October 14, 1929: "I am sorry you are broke. You always are broke unless at a time when I have just given you money. Your interests have absorbed all the cash and credit you can get, and threaten to absorb mine. But, nothing doing anymore, my dear. It's more important to me that I buy the stuff I want and take the trips I plan, than for you to buy this and that for investment. . . . I earn most of the money, and I intend to have more to say about its use. So, that's that. As to the future, of course if I do not go ahead with my plans, we'll have no need to bother our heads about money."

Two weeks later the New York Stock Exchange plummeted, and America, the world, and the life of Zane Grey would never be the same. But despite the eventual failure of half the banks in the country and a miserable unemployment rate of 30 percent, Zane and Dolly were able to weather the Great Depression without any loss of their enthusiasm for life. A notable feature that came out of the economic downturn was that the Western inspired a generation to survive and endure the times. With the arrival of sound in movies, a host of new actors and actresses were primed for the next epoch of the Western, including plans for the third version of *Riders of the Purple Sage*.

CHAPTER TEN

Riders Redux

BY 1930 AND WITH THE WIDE POPULARITY OF SOUND FILMS, FOX FILM Corporation started prepping a whole new era of Zane Grey features. Some stars of the earlier Grey films did not make the successful transition to "talkies." These actors included William Farnum, Dustin Farnum, Mary Mersch, Richard Dix, Tom Mix, and Mabel Ballin. Some of them, including the Farnum brothers, found work in supporting roles. Fox, however, groomed several new talents for major roles, including Myrna Loy, Lucille Brown, Noah Beery, Cecilia Parker, George O'Brien, and Marguerite Churchill.

O'Brien as Lassiter and Churchill as Jane Withersteen combined to make the 1931 version of *Riders of the Purple Sage* one of the best screen adaptations. Born in San Francisco in 1899, O'Brien was the son of the city's police chief and gained prominence as a heavyweight boxer in World War I. He was always athletic and had massive upper-body strength, which led one director to forever label him as "the chest." A chance encounter with Tom Mix led to an interview and later a job with Fox Film Corporation. For several years after World War I, O'Brien worked as a stuntman and extra in several Westerns. In 1924 John Ford handpicked him for the role of Davy Brandon in the seminal film *The Iron Trail*, and from that point on, he was starring in a parade of films for Fox.

O'Brien's strength as an actor lay in his range and versatility. He could play heavy dramatic roles in a variety of genres and then switch to lighter romantic comedies. On the set he was an exuberant performer and jokester. A director once called him "a man of a few thousand words." When sound films became standard fare, he acted in Westerns almost exclusively. In 1930, he starred as Buck Duane in Zane Grey's *The Lone Star Ranger*. Filmed in Monument Valley and directed by A. F. Erickson, the movie launched O'Brien on a track that included him in some of the best Western films of the 1930s.

In 1930, he reprised his role as Buck Duane in director Alfred Werker's *The Last of the Duanes*. O'Brien showed up for shooting the movie in Sedona beginning in March and continuing through May of 1930. His costars were veteran Myrna Loy and Lucille Brown in her film debut. Production crews erected an elaborate outdoor set near Sedona's Battlement Mesa at a cost of $50,000, which included a dirt street composed of houses, bunkhouses, a dry goods store, a blacksmith shop, a corral, and an Indian hogan. Fox wanted to avoid the label of B Western as much as possible, so his set designers created an authentic period village. It was also used the following year for director Hamilton MacFadden's *Riders of the Purple Sage*.

Along with Lone Pine, Monument Valley, the Grand Canyon, and the Vermillion Cliffs, Sedona, Arizona, became one of the premier filming locations for Westerns. Its serrated buttes and red-banded cliffs could easily pass for the remote arroyos around the Grand Canyon and southern Utah. But Sedona had an additional advantage. It was near enough to Los Angeles for film crews to reach fairly quickly and yet remote enough to appear pristine and untrammeled. With its valleys filled with pine and juniper and its pillared rock formations majestic against the sky, Sedona remained an ideal location for decades. Unlike most sites in the western United States, Sedona could not easily be duplicated, which further added to its singular reputation. Grey considered it Surprise Valley writ large.

In March of 1931, the set used for *The Last of the Duanes* was busy once again, as MacFadden and the Fox production team moved in for the filming of *Riders of the Purple Sage*, starring George O'Brien and a young leading lady named Marguerite Churchill. At the time of filming, Churchill was barely twenty years old. The previous year she had made her Western film debut with a youthful guy named John Wayne. That movie, of course, was Raoul Walsh's *The Big Trail*, and it was Wayne's first starring role; it was Churchill's eighth feature film.

Along with Lone Pine, Sedona became one of the premier filming locations for Hollywood Westerns. It was the setting for the third adaptation of *Riders*, starring George O'Brien.

ARLENE WALLER @SHUTTERSTOCK.COM

Churchill's role beside John Wayne in *The Big Trail* enabled her to be more selective in future films, and since she liked the character of Jane Withersteen in Grey's novel, she expressed interest in playing her. After MacFadden cast her as Withersteen, she arrived in Sedona and immersed herself in the character.

A 1925 graduate of Harvard, MacFadden worked in community theater before joining Fox as a director. He was part of that generation who were formally trained in acting, screenwriting, and production. *Riders of the Purple Sage* was his first Western, and he took some novel steps with it. In an early scene, as Venters (James Todd) is in the tight grasp of the marauding gang, MacFadden shoots a close-up of him. Venters sees a solitary gunman approaching and then drawing his gun. "It's *Lassiter!*" cries Venters, and we know we are in the presence of the fabled Texas Ranger. MacFadden also had photographer George Schneiderman film a stampeding herd, up close, from a speeding truck. Later, the photographer filmed, from the same truck, Lassiter chasing down the rider who steals Black Star and Night. Advancements in film quality enabled Schneiderman to capture foreground terrain as well as background scenery in much sharper focus.

The Mormon theme was completely dropped in favor of a more familiar conflict, that of the ranch owner (Withersteen) being harassed by land grabbers and cattle rustlers. The Law and Order League, as it was known, was merely a front for Judge Dyer and his gang of thugs. Tull and Oldring were back to sneer and snarl in all their nefarious glory.

The script, written by Barry Conners and Philip Stein, eliminated Grey's swallowtail plot and concentrated solely on the movements of Jane and Lassiter. The Bess and Venters storyline was woven into the primary plot. The entrance into Surprise Valley was only suggested. Lassiter's shove of Balancing Rock was retained, as well as Bess and Venters's flight to avoid capture.

Westerns of the era had a running time of sixty minutes, which eliminated most of Grey's strength as an author. Screenwriters pared novels down to their essentials. By the wayside went Grey's evocative descriptions of desert and pillared cliffs, his need to get inside his characters' minds and lives, his devotion to nature, and his ability to render the loneliness of the wanderers of the West. The ultimate goal of Westerns was to entertain, and anything that slowed the pace of the action was carelessly extracted.

Despite these limitations, the screen duo of O'Brien and Churchill ignited the storyline and made this version of *Riders* the best of the Fox studio productions. The spirited O'Brien transformed the traditional film version of Lassiter from a stoic gunfighter and horseman into a man capable of a relationship with a young woman. Churchill played a very poised and self-assured Jane Withersteen, giving the character a more stubborn side than previous films had. At the age of twenty, Churchill gave no hint of being a novice among professional actors. Perhaps adding to the onscreen chemistry of the two was the fact that during filming O'Brien and Churchill had fallen in love. They were married three years later.

Evidently, the critics were pleased with O'Brien and Churchill's performances in *Riders of the Purple Sage*. The *New York Times* noted: "Here the players look as though they belonged to the times, which is more than can be said for those who figured in mute versions of this narrative. Stalwart Mr. O'Brien is thoroughly in his element, both as a rider and an actor."

Variety added that "this Zane Grey milestone is still a good Western. ... O'Brien interprets Lassiter as the familiar strong and silent type. It's a likable performance by the featured player whose dexterity with a gun is noteworthy here."[1]

As soon as he finished filming *Riders*, O'Brien headed to the Grand Canyon to begin shooting *The Rainbow Trail*. O'Brien went on to make several more popular Westerns based on Zane Grey's work, including *Robbers' Roost* and *The Last Trail*. Throughout the 1930s, he was always among the highest paid Western actors in Hollywood. George was always a man of action. When World War II broke out in late 1941, he volunteered for active duty, serving in nearly every major offensive in the Pacific Theater. He remained close to John Ford, who also served in the Pacific, as a filmmaker. After the war, as acting roles dried up, Ford cast O'Brien in several of his Western epics, including *Fort Apache*, *She Wore a Yellow Ribbon*, and *Cheyenne Autumn*.

* * *

By 1930, with the widespread popularity of radio, books, and film, *Riders of the Purple Sage* was the most famous Western tale, even overshadowing *The Virginian* and Emerson Hough's *The Covered Wagon*. The main reason for his success was that during those early years Zane Grey kept writing. Beginning with the appearance of *The Heritage of the Desert* in 1910, he maintained a steady stream of Western novels that kept him in the forefront of readers' minds. Even unsung authors of the period, such as Ernest Haycox and Alan LeMay, and veterans like Max Brand profited from the standard set by the great author of the West.

Culture was saturated with Western archetypes. There were the traditional heroes wearing white Stetsons and riding acrobatic steeds. But now there was abundant singing in Western movies, and also plenty of yodeling, plucking, strumming, picking, whistling, and harmonizing. The era of the musical cowpoke had arrived. In the mid-1930s, singer and songwriter Bob Nolan helped formed the Sons of the Pioneers and gave Westerns a new musical element. Gene Autry and Roy Rogers were only part of the "singing cowboy" trend in movies. All in all, the West seemed like a happy place, far from the worries of the common, and perhaps, unemployed wage earner. As the relentless clouds of dust ruined crops and livelihoods, the intensity of Western music increased.

Many heroes wanted to be at the top of the pack. There were advertisements for the "King of the Cowboys" or the "World's Greatest Cowboy" in theater lobby cards. In the tradition of Black Star and Night, great horses galloped and leaped across the screen: Silver, Trigger, Black Jack, Champion, Tony, Cactus, and Raider. And riding them were statuesque men of the range, as well as "kids": Billy the Kid, the Durango Kid, and the Ringo Kid.

In an age of "come one, come all," the romantic phase of both A and B (budget) Westerns lasted into the 1940s and beyond, making stars of Gary Cooper, John Wayne, Henry Fonda, Myrna Loy, and Randolph Scott.

*   *   *

In 1936 Fox Films merged with Twentieth Century Pictures to form Twentieth Century Fox. Most of the production staff and actors from William Fox's original company were retained, including the well-established directors John Ford and Fritz Lang. By this time Ford had moved into the A list of film directors, although most of his films in the late silent era to the sound movies were not Westerns. As a writer and director for Fox and RKO Pictures, he had made several critically important films such as *The Lost Patrol* (1934) and *The Informer* (1935). He resumed his focus on Westerns in 1936 with *The Last Outlaw*, which he helped to write. From that point on Ford rose to become one of the top ten directors in Hollywood. He vetted his film proposals carefully, weeding out ones he thought banal and focusing on those that his instinct and talent could develop into important films. In 1939 he discovered Monument Valley, the scene of so many Zane Grey Westerns, and both the place and John Ford would never be the same. The product was *Stagecoach*, the seminal film of the realist movement in Western filmmaking, which was nominated for seven 1940 Academy Awards, including Best Picture and Best Director. Screenwriter Dudley Nichols adapted the script for *Stagecoach* from Ernest Haycox's 1937 short story "The Stage to Lordsburg."

In 1937, Fox began grooming a twenty-one-year-old stuntman from Montana named George Montgomery. Montgomery played in several uncredited roles in B Westerns in the late 1930s starring Roy Rogers, Gene Autry, and John Wayne. His first starring role came in 1941 when he played opposite Mary Beth Hughes in *The Cowboy and the Blonde*. Fox scheduled two Zane Grey Westerns for production, *The Last of the Duanes* and the fourth adaptation of *Riders of the Purple Sage*. Montgomery was chosen for the lead roles in each from a field of ten actors that included Henry Fonda.

Mary Howard, whose most recent film was *Billy the Kid*, playing opposite Robert Taylor, starred as Jane. The studio selected James Tinling to direct the fourth version of *Riders*. Tinling was widely regarded as the best second-feature director in Fox's stable. He chose the Anchor Ranch and the Alabama Hills in Lone Pine for the setting, which by the 1940s had become so popular for a filming location that it was in operation twelve months a year. Tinling and screenwriter William Bruckner thought it wise to exclude the Mormon theme and emphasize a less contentious one. Consequently, Elder Tull does not appear in the film. Judge Dyer and his son Adam are villains in league with Oldring and his Masked Rider.

Zane and his animal companion in Arizona

Although it does not compete with Fox's 1931 film starring George O'Brien, the Tinling-Montgomery film offers several advancements, including sharper film resolution and better sound. Montgomery appears more aloof than the gregarious O'Brien, and the Sierra Nevada backgrounds recall the Tom Mix version of 1925. *Variety* (October 20, 1941) reported that "this old Zane Grey story, written for a former generation and already filmed three times by Fox, may be considered creaky in plot or dated, but alongside much of the Western stuff that is turned out today, it's still okay. Story contains more than an adequate amount of action, and in addition to moving at a sprightly pace, maintains good suspense. Twentieth has given the film an above-average production."

Despite all his achievements in the Western novel and all his friendships with Hollywood producers, Zane Grey took only a mild interest in the third and fourth adaptations of his 1912 novel. He celebrated his sixty-seventh birthday on January 31, 1939. He was deep-sea fishing in Australia and eyed beating his own world record catch of a 1,036-pound tiger shark three years earlier. He planned to cruise the Australian coast near the Great Barrier Reef before heading home to California in May. He ended a letter to Dolly by saying: "This is written in a hurry to tell you how happy your letter made me and how much I love you, and how I am about well again, and everything is fine."[2] By the time he headed northwest across the equator toward California, he had written and published forty-six novels, most of which had become Fox or Paramount Pictures productions.

As early as 1936, Zane had experienced signs of physical decline. The strenuous life had seemingly caught up with him, and this translated into a weakened mental state. From Wyoming, on June 2 of that year, he comments to Dolly: "Something is wrong with me. I don't care a damn. I don't have a thrill. I am not excited over the extraordinary scenery. I have gone about the business as always, except I haven't the old something. It makes me sick to realize it. . . . My great trouble is that I cannot sleep, or if I do, I awaken and have morbid thoughts. . . . I do get a thrill out of the possibility of Harper's contract for my westerns, and other stories, too. But how am I to create the stories—and write them, without that something? This is the inevitable toll of the years. . . . But I do feel young, and even that is an illusion. I know I can write better than I ever could. That is the hell of it."

That summer, Grey reached down to tie his shoe and realized he could not grasp the lace. After several attempts, he finally tied his shoe. He walked to a hammock and lay down, and after several minutes discerned that he had no feeling in his right leg. He rose and tried to walk but fell a couple of times on one knee. His speech became slurred, and some friends rushed to his aid.

The next morning, a doctor declared that Zane had suffered a paralytic stroke caused by severely constricted arteries.

Three years later, after several journeys abroad, he spent the summer and fall in Altadena with Dolly, occasionally fishing on Catalina Island. At seven-thirty in the morning of October 23, 1939, he exercised on the veranda of his home, toweled himself off, and made it to the bedroom before collapsing on the floor. After suffering a heart attack, he died that morning with Dolly by his side.

* * *

The West may have lost its greatest writer of romantic sagas, but the reading public had many more years of Grey stories to enjoy. Harper and Brothers had enough stockpiled to release one a year through 1963. Moreover, Hollywood continued to film some of his more important works. But it was television that became the most important beneficiary of his stories.

Over fifty years would pass before the release of the fifth adaptation of *Riders of the Purple Sage*, in 1996. During the years of World War II and immediately thereafter, the Western began changing from a vehicle of pure entertainment to a more serious investigation of the people and events that marked the halcyon years of 1865–1910 in the Old West. A new generation of readers and filmgoers, some of whom had never heard of *Riders of the Purple Sage*, began setting the trends in the genre. Zane Grey's romantic melodramas did not fit in with the demands of this new era in filmmaking.

The shift was toward greater realism in film, and this trend was largely steered by the established directors and writers of the time, who made the period between 1945 and 1960 one of the greats in Western cinema.

In his later years, Zane could be found in his favorite Morris chair in his den festooned with Western memorabilia.

Directors John Ford, Raoul Walsh, John Huston, Howard Hawks, Fred Zinnemann, and George Stevens helmed some of the best Westerns ever.

Of the good movies of the period, there emerged several notable ones, including Hawks's *Red River*, Huston's *The Treasure of the Sierra Madre*, Ford's *Fort Apache* and *She Wore a Yellow Ribbon*, Zinnemann's *High Noon*, and Stevens's *Shane*. New novelists such as Louis L'Amour (*Hondo*) and Jack Schaefer (*Shane*) joined screenwriters Frank Nugent, Dudley Nichols, Carl Foreman, and Alan LeMay in transforming the mythical West into a form compelling to the present generation.

Since Owen Wister's *The Virginian* and Zane Grey's *Riders of the Purple Sage*, the popular Western had kept a steady and, at times, predictable course. From Dustin Farnum and William S. Hart to George Montgomery and John Wayne, and through a devastating war and stock market collapse to a crippling economic depression, the form had developed into an American institution. But on the eve of another world war, the Western was to undergo another major change. In 1940, with the publication of Walter van Tilburg Clark's *The Ox-Bow Incident*, Zane Grey's West of unflappable cowboys and picturesque backdrops shifted into a realistic phase of spiteful vigilantes and impromptu lynching parties. This became apparent to theatergoers in May 1943, when William Wellman's stark, cheerless film *The Ox–Bow Incident*, starring Henry Fonda, premiered in New York City.

The film is set in rural Nevada in 1885. Two drifters, Gil Carter (Henry Fonda) and Art Croft (Harry Morgan), arrive in Bridger's Wells and head for the saloon. The locals in the saloon talk of cattle rustling in the area and why such thieves are lower than scum. With everyone fueled by whiskey, one of the themes of *The Ox-Bow Incident* is set: the mob is already primed for action against cattle rustlers—guilty or not.

Rumor spreads throughout the saloon that a man named Kincaid has been murdered and his cattle stolen. Art and Gil are soon swept up in the fervor. They willingly join a posse to help track down and punish the killers and cattle thieves.

Director William Wellman and screenwriter Lamar Trotti never let the action degenerate into a B Western revenge story, or a "let's head 'em off at the pass" melodrama. All actions and conversations have plausible motivation, and the characters act in accordance with their primal instincts.

The posse soon reaches Ox-Bow canyon, where they encounter three suspicious strangers dozing in their bedrolls: a well-educated man (Dana Andrews), a Mexican man (Anthony Quinn), and an elderly man (Frances Ford). The cattle, presumably stolen by the three, linger nearby.

After the strangers cannot produce a bill of sale for the cattle, the posse begins to discuss the fate of the interlopers. A part of the group wants to bring the three men to trial in town. Another, more strident part of the mob, led by Confederate veteran Major Tetley, urges them to hang the men immediately. As the posse debates the men's fate, the argument seesaws back and forth among the posse members, some voting for a reasonable and just solution and others demanding quick punishment for the suspicious trio.

In the end, the more thunderous voices prevail and the men are lynched. Only later, on their return to town, do the posse members learn that Kincaid is alive and that the men who shot and wounded him have been arrested. The saloon settles into glum silence as the men succumb to overpowering guilt about what they have done.

Wellman's film is unsparing in its attack on brute force, quick judgment, and the power of authority to sway the moral beliefs of the most staunchly principled people in any given situation. Clark's novel and Wellman's film also demonstrate how any group, town, or nation can immediately become suspicious of outsiders, and therefore end up becoming more insulated and reckless in their decisions and actions, ultimately leading to paranoia and destruction.

Wellman's canvas does not contain the scenic landscapes of Zane Grey and other romanticists. It is dark, stony, denuded of life. Ox-Bow Canyon is Golgotha without the crosses. Wellman casts the hanging scene with shadowed, eerie light evocative of the portentous moment at hand. The hangman's ropes dangle from a gaunt, leafless oak tree like the strings of marionettes waiting for the action to begin. It is no wonder Fox studio executives held their breath before its release: this was not their fathers' or grandfathers' film of yodeling cowboys and happy trails. *The Ox-Bow Incident* was the precursor of the existentialist Western film noir, one of the forerunners of the novels of Cormac McCarthy and the movies of Clint Eastwood (who claimed that *Ox-Bow* is his favorite film). But it also gave new life to the Western, which for so long had been moldering without any clear direction.

The Ox-Bow Incident was never considered a controversial film for the time. Indeed, most observers felt such a version of the West was long overdue. It was filmed during the summer of 1942, but Fox producers withheld its debut, fearing the movie's somber themes would cripple its success. Although it was never a blockbuster, *The Ox-Bow Incident* influenced the genre for the next few years. The initial reviews for its 1943 debut were predictably mixed. The *New York Times* reported that it "is not a picture that will cheer or brighten your day. But it is one which, for sheer, stark drama, is currently hard to beat."[3] The *New Yorker*, rather lamely, called it "a good piece of work." A reviewer for *Harrison Reports* remarked that the film "was a dark, depressing, at times, horrible melodrama." Twentieth Century Fox president Darryl F. Zanuck considered the work a financial flop, even while praising the film as one of the best of the year.

Less than a decade later, Stanley Kramer's production of *High Noon* (1952), also released by Twentieth Century Fox, entered similar uncharted territory and became—however innocently—the most controversial Western of the era. Not many Hollywood insiders could have predicted that a movie featuring a stalwart Gary Cooper facing down four killers would produce such alarm throughout the country.

The Ox-Bow Incident had been released during the depths of the Second World War, and the themes in the film reflected the country's struggle with totalitarian regimes in Germany and Italy. *High Noon* emerged at a time when the Communist scare in America reached a fever pitch, and the film and its writer, Carl Foreman, had to battle on two fronts: first, with the studio to get it produced, and second, with politically motivated critics who sought to smear his name.

The film itself, starring Gary Cooper and Grace Kelly, is a gem of concentrated directing and screenwriting. It is told in real time. The actual time in the film consumes one hour and forty minutes (after editing), as the clock ticks away to high noon. The more concentrated the time, the stronger the suspense. In fact, time becomes the central feature of the film, with a pendulum clock hammering out the seconds and marking time to the frantic heartbeats of Marshal Will Kane.

The movie opens one Sunday morning at 10:35 in Hadleyville, New Mexico Territory, circa 1870. Marshal Kane is marrying his Quaker sweetheart and about to leave the town for a new life elsewhere. After the ceremony, word reaches Kane and the townspeople that Frank Miller, a hardened killer whom Kane sent to prison years ago, is arriving on the noon train and is gunning for the marshal. Already, three of Miller's saddle tramps have gathered at the depot to await his arrival. After much deliberation, Kane decides to stay and fight it out. He seeks help from the men of the hamlet and collects a small group of deputies. But as time quickly passes and nerves fray, they one by one back out, leaving Kane to encounter the four killers in the streets of the town. Even his new bride decides to leave.

Amy Kane (Grace Kelly) is frightened by these sudden developments and left facing a moral quandary as deep as her husband's. Does she obey her religious beliefs, as Jane Withersteen tried to obey hers, and renounce gun violence? Does she seek out the advice of Kane's former girlfriend in town? Can she run far away from Hadleyville? Or, can she resolve her moral dilemma by believing in her husband? Carl Foreman delivers a solid script by creating characters who have to make the greatest decisions of their lives—and then giving them fifty-nine minutes in which to make them.

Foreman based his screenplay on John Cunningham's 1947 short story "The Tin Star," which was published in *Collier's* magazine. He brought his idea to fellow producer Stanley Kramer, and both agreed at the time to move forward with the project. After filming, in late 1951, Foreman was brought before the House Committee on Un-American Activities and accused of being a Communist sympathizer. Wishing to avoid the taint that an accusation might bring to the release of the film, Kramer slowly started minimizing Foreman's role as producer. Foreman fled to England, and by the time the film was released in early 1952, he had been blacklisted in Hollywood. Foreman, as screenwriter, received lavish praise for the film and eventually an Academy Award nomination. But the guilt-by-association stigma hung over his role as producer, and

Kramer, a socially conscious executive, quietly eliminated Foreman from that position.[4]

All of this chicanery had nothing to do with the intrinsic merit of the film. It is a taut Western thriller and remains a classic. The film's director, Fred Zinnemann, used Foreman's script and shot the film in black and white to sustain maximum drama. *High Noon* gave stature and respectability to the genre and was often labeled "the Western for people who don't like Westerns." The Joseph McCarthy era instilled such paranoia in the general populace that the film became open to several interpretations. Some filmgoers saw it as an allegory of the common man being stripped of his rights while the rest of the world lapses into complacency. Others had their own opinions, including John Wayne and director Howard Hawks, who both contended that frontier men and women would not shirk from supporting their outgunned marshal. Wayne went on to call the film "un-American."

Led by the curmudgeonly but incisive film critic Bosley Crowther of the *New York Times,* reviews of *High Noon* came in quickly and favorably. Crowther called Zinnemann's movie "a sure illumination of the human character . . . Like most works of art, it is simple—simple in the structure of its plot and comparatively simple in the layout of its fundamental issues and morals. . . . How Mr. Foreman has surrounded this simple and forceful tale with tremendous dramatic implications is a thing we cannot glibly state in words. It is a matter of skill in movie-writing, but, more than that, it is the putting down, in terms of visually simplified images, a pattern of poetic ideas." Crowther concluded by saying: "Meaningful in its implications, as well as loaded with interest and suspense, *High Noon* is a Western to challenge *Stagecoach* for the all-time championship."[5]

Many observers offered their own opinions about the true meaning of the film. Quite possibly, it was a well-written, well-directed, and well-acted film about a man in a drowsy New Mexico town who stands up to four unhinged killers. The need to call a film "allegorical" may be an invitation to miss its greatness entirely. As D. H. Lawrence observed: "Trust the tale and not the teller." In any case, *High Noon* proved that a Western was capable of as much suspense as any Hitchcock psychological thriller. It went on to snare seven Academy Award nominations and four wins, including the Oscars for Best Actor (Cooper) and Best Music (Dimitri Tiomkin's haunting musical score).

Fox and Paramount Pictures were the primary studios for developing and filming Zane Grey Westerns into the 1940s, but by the next decade RKO, United Artists, and Republic Pictures joined the duo. The demand for Zane Grey feature films was reaching its end by 1956, resulting in Republic's *The Maverick Queen*, featuring Barbara Stanwyck and Barry Sullivan, one of the last Grey films to reach the screen.

But if Zane Grey's feature films were reaching a conclusion, his influence on the Western was only strengthening. In 1953, Paramount began developing Jack Schaefer's 1949 novel *Shane*. Seasoned director George Stevens (*Gunga Din, A Place in the Sun*) helmed the production, and Pulitzer Prize-winning writer A. B. Guthrie (*The Way West*) adapted Schaefer's novel for the screen.

On the face of it, *Shane* appears to revive the traditional thematic features of a gunfighter involved in a range war, features that marked Grey's *Heritage of the Desert* and *Riders of the Purple Sage*, as well as numerous early Westerns. A mysterious gunman named Shane rides into the lives of a Wyoming homesteader in conflict with a resentful land baron and his minions. Shane seeks to bury his past as a man of the gun, but the villainous men in his midst won't let him.

George Stevens, along with John Ford, Fred Zinnemann, and Howard Hawks, shaped the cinematic Western in the 1950s. Stevens, in particular, brought an unusual sensitivity and worldly experience to the filming of Westerns, taking a rather conventional plot structure like *Shane* and turning it into a small masterpiece. Stevens came up through the ranks of directors in the 1930s, overseeing everything from screwball and slapstick comedies to Westerns and costume dramas. During the Second World War, as a lieutenant colonel in the US Army Signal Corps, he directed the filming of the D-Day landings in Normandy, the American forces' entry into Paris, and the liberation of the Dachau concentration camp, a haunting experience that gave him a profound understanding of human suffering.

His postwar work reflected this awareness of the breadth of the human condition. Stevens won his first Oscar for directing Montgomery

Clift and Elizabeth Taylor in *A Place in the Sun* in 1951. In *Shane* he sought a fresh approach to the traditional Western. To get the type of screenplay he wanted, he turned to Guthrie, who pared down Schaefer's novel into a fast-paced and lively script. After Stevens's first choices for the lead role—Montgomery Clift and William Holden—were confirmed to be on other projects, he chose Alan Ladd to star opposite Jean Arthur.

Like Schaefer, George Stevens wished to show a truer West than that of Zane Grey. Stevens had worked on a few Zane Grey short films in the 1920s, but now he was ready to advance the Western to another level. His choice of Ladd in the lead role raised some controversy among studio executives. Ladd, it was agreed, was no John Wayne, Gary Cooper, or William Holden. Ladd had played some strong roles in the 1940s but now was heading into the sunset of his career. At five foot, six inches, he lacked the stature of other major actors in Westerns of the period. But Stevens liked him for the same qualities he saw in Clift, namely his vulnerability and sensitivity for the role of Shane. He may have been no Wayne or Cooper, but Ladd had a sturdy enough screen presence to give Shane the strength, resolve, and credibility the character required.

One of the first frames of the movie shows Ladd on horseback meeting the Starretts (Van Heflin and Jean Arthur) on their ranch in Wyoming. Stevens filmed the scene from near ground level, which elevated the characters to a kind of magisterial presence against the serrated white peaks of the Tetons in the background. From that scene on, there was no doubt that Ladd was the right man for the role.

Coming off the success of *High Noon* the year before, *Shane* provided *New York Times* reviewer Bosley Crowther with a near embarrassment of riches for the contemporary Western. Crowther was drawn to the apparent simplicity of Stevens's film. "*Shane* contains something more than beauty and grandeur of the mountains and plains, drenched by the brilliant Western sunshine and the violent, torrential, black-browed rains. It contains a tremendous comprehension of the bitterness and passion of the feuds that existed between the homesteaders and the cattlemen on the open range. It contains a disturbing revelation of the savagery that prevailed in the hearts of the old gun-fighters, who were simply legal killers under the frontier code."[6]

The film was more recently reviewed by Roger Ebert, who remained fascinated by Shane's character. "There is a little of the samurai in him," remarked Ebert, "and the medieval knight. He has a code. And yet—there is something else suggested by his behavior, his personality, his whole tone. Here is man tough enough to handle any threat and handsome enough to win the heart of almost any woman. Why does he present himself as a weakling? . . . There must be a deep current of fear, enlivened by masochism. Is he afraid of women? Maybe. Does he deliberately lead men to think they can manhandle them, and then kill them? Manifestly. Does he do this out of bravery and courage, and because he believes in doing the right thing? That is the conventional wisdom. . . . *Shane* never says, and maybe never knows."[7]

With superb acting, directing, and writing, *Shane* is a film greater than the sum of its parts, and therein, between the lines, in the poetic frontier images, and in the unusually nuanced character of the man named Shane, dwells the movie's enduring qualities.

* * *

By the end of the twentieth century, movie audiences were quite accustomed to psychological, heartless, sociological, slapstick, anti-heroic, homicidal, and revisionist Westerns. So how could a Hollywood producer adapt Zane Grey's romance novel in an age of realism? Well, by adapting Grey's romance novel in an age of realism. One of the few ways a producer could get *Riders of the Purple Sage* into production was to script it for the small screen. The commercial Western was often too risky for wide circulation, so producer Norman Rosemont decided to approach Turner Network Television (TNT) with the idea of reviving the exploits of Jim Lassiter, Jane Withersteen, Bern Venters, and Elizabeth Erne for contemporary television audiences. The process became a ten-year journey comprising several dead ends; it wasn't until the early 1990s that TNT agreed to proceed with the production.

Rosemont also sought out the husband-and-wife team of Ed Harris and Amy Madigan and, together with scriptwriter Gill Dennis, director

Charles Haid, and cinematographer William Wages, spurred the project into production. This 1996 adaptation, the fifth version of *Riders of the Purple Sage*, stands up very well and demonstrates that Grey's 1912 novel has enough stamina for the modern age. Also starring Henry Thomas as Bern Venters and newcomer Robin Tunney in her fourth outing, the film owes much to its Moab, Utah, backgrounds and the sere surrounding countryside. Dennis penned a spartan script for Harris and Madigan's romance to unfold, grow, and mature against the sinister atmosphere and unforgiving badlands around Cottonwoods.

Harris plays a magnificent Lassiter: tough, honest, and honorable, less jocular than George O'Brien, but still a man of the wasteland who looks like he has sprouted between the sage and mesquite. Some of the more obvious mannerisms and diction of 1912 have been eliminated. The operatic coos and hand-over-the-heart reactions, so evident in the early films, have also been dropped. More modern approaches to *Riders* have emphasized the drained, earthy qualities of the soil surrounding the characters. The great open spaces around Lassiter and Jane that stretch to the hogbacks and mesas of Moab have as much silence and majesty as the frequent pauses in their conversations. This contemporary approach to *Riders of the Purple Sage* makes the storyline more credible and further enhances the immortal quality of the tale.

Some directors prefer not to work with married couples in lead roles, but Harris and Madigan, wed since 1983, were among the first to express interest in reviving Grey's classic. Their onscreen presence recalls the relationship of O'Brien and Churchill from the 1931 Fox production. Madigan as Jane raises the character's complexity to a new level. Partly as a result of women's changing roles over the years, she plays Withersteen as an assertive widow trying to maintain Cottonwoods while members of her church continue to terrorize her. But the simple fact is that Madigan's portrayal and Zane Grey's 1912 depiction of Jane are relatively similar. It was only the conventions of the film industry that represented Jane Withersteen as a somewhat fragile, immature landowner.

The one drawback of the 1996 film is the reluctance of cinematographer William Wages to take full advantage of the countryside. The film was shot in several locations, including Moab, the Vermillion Cliffs, and the Kaibab National Forest in Arizona. The backgrounds are adequate and beautiful, but filmmakers need to take the landscape of *Riders* into account. This could have been accomplished during the opening credits. In the film, we see a rider (Madigan) with a few horses in tow, galloping across an indistinct landscape while a shimmering sun crosses the sky. This would be the time for the riders of the purple sage to make their entry and simultaneously reveal the distinctive shapes and colors of the terrain. Zane Grey's verbal sketches need the filmmaker's compelling photographic images for the story to have its maximum impact.

Dennis's screenplay follows the novel's storyline near faithfully. The members of the Mormon community in the novel are replaced by an insular band of religious zealots. Director Charles Haid never lets the story slip into melodrama, shaping it into a scene-by-scene crescendo until Lassiter, guns ablaze, seeks his revenge.

Ratings for the movie were stellar, and the reviews also were glowing. *TV Guide* remarked that *Riders* "maintains a full gallop by humanizing its genre-ready characters. If *Riders* is flawed, it's due to the expository glitches in the retelling of Millie's complicated history and the screenplay's failure to give the Bern-Bess subplot the same weight applied to the redemptive love between Jane and Lassiter. . . . Fiercely acted sans showy histrionics by Madigan and Harris, the Jane-Lassiter relationship is one of the most complex to be found in the genre; one doesn't encounter this kind of equal partnership in a John Ford Western. . . . *Riders* presents characters whose life-and-death revelations are accessible to contemporary audiences without having to rely on an anachronistic veneer of modern psychology."[8]

This fifth adaptation of Grey's classic novel came nearly sixty years after the author's death. For a literary work of any kind to survive and remain popular for that length of time is something of a rarity.

The Western as an art form, however, was in decline. The readers who devoured books and the filmgoers who sat in theaters were diminishing with each passing year. Publishers that previously groomed and promoted Western authors were folding or merging into conglomerates. The West that initially had been part of the lifeblood of American culture seemed to be withering in the winds of change. Grey's purple sage still spread throughout the Southwest, but too often it was cluttered with plastic bags and gum wrappers. The West was suffering from a lack of life.

After the 1996 film, it might have appeared to most observers that Zane Grey's tale of love and defiance would sink into the dust of the century's end, but not to American composer Craig Bohmler. He was among a group of believers who was willing to give *Riders of the Purple Sage* new life. But this time, a new adaptation of the novel did not originate in New York or on the West Coast. It originated where it all began nearly a hundred years earlier.

Way out there.

Epilogue

Riders, Ride On!

It might seem odd—if not slightly absurd—for someone to consider mounting an important musical about the West while living in the heart of the Arizona desert. But for some daring entrepreneurs, that's exactly what transpired.

Although Phoenix is now a sprawling, cosmopolitan city, it was once a grubby village where the stagecoach from Wickenburg rolled in during the afternoon, and where just to the north Geronimo and his band of Apaches outfoxed the US Army patrols in the chaparral-covered hills. Today, as steel cages rise into an impatient sun and fingers of the city reach out to grab the remaining portions of land, Phoenix has no trouble remembering its Wild West heritage.

Against this backdrop, musician Craig Bohmler attempted to channel the voices of Arizona's past. In 2010, he took a rather leisurely drive from Phoenix up through the Tonto Forest, intending on hiking along the way. After encountering a torrential cloudburst, he took shelter in a remote cabin near Payson. The cabin/museum turned out to be an exact replica of the shelter Zane Grey used for his sojourns in Arizona. The original was destroyed by forest fire in 1991.

Such a port in the storm provided Bohmler with a personal connection to the best-selling writer. He went home, pulled out a copy of *Riders of the Purple Sage*, and realized that its hyperbole and melodrama would make a fine opera. Opera? In America? If you asked most residents of the United States to name an opera by an American composer, they would remain speechless. Although opera has never enjoyed the interest and popularity in America as it has in Europe, it has had a loyal following throughout the years. It is frequently confused with musical theater, and the line between the two is often blurred. In and of itself, American opera has a distinguished lineage, beginning, perhaps most famously, with George Gershwin's *Porgy and Bess* in 1935. This landmark English-language opera, often described as a folk opera, reached deep into the roots of African American culture and produced several well-known songs such as "Summertime."

In the late nineteenth century, opera houses proliferated throughout the American West. As westward expansion increased, families wanted a decent place to witness European operas, made famous by Verdi, Mozart, Rossini, Bizet, and Puccini. Opera houses became the cultural centers of town, frequently placed between the saloon and dance halls, and around the corner from the library and the blacksmith. Towns invited celebrities like Oscar Wilde and Mark Twain to introduce the great operas of Europe, adding a distinguished touch to the reputation of their communities.

The West provided composers with themes that otherwise might have been overlooked. Commissioned by the Metropolitan Opera for its premiere in 1910, Puccini's *Girl of the Golden West* might very well be the most acclaimed opera about Western culture of the nineteenth century. Author of towering works such as *Tosca* and *Madama Butterfly*, Puccini adapted American author David Belasco's play (of the same name) for *Girl of the Golden West*. Although it is rendered in Italian, the opera features characteristic if romantic scenes of a California gold camp of the 1850s. Puccini considered *Girl of the Golden West* one of his greatest works, and its influence can be seen in numerous American operas of the twentieth century.

As the century advanced, opera and musical theater matured like twin sisters, although the latter proved more popular and commercially successful. The selective use of Western themes and motifs helped make Rodgers and Hammerstein's *Oklahoma!* (1943) a revolutionary musical for its time. *Oklahoma's* music, choreography, and book proved so noteworthy that it was awarded its own special Pulitzer Prize. On its heels came Irving Berlin's *Annie Get Your Gun* and, in 1951, Alan Lerner and Frederick Loewe's *Paint Your Wagon*. All three musicals were smash Broadway hits as well as successful films.

In addition to musicals, ballet mined some of the resources of Western folklore. One of America's great composers, Aaron Copland, broke fresh ground with his 1938 ballet *Billy the Kid*, which featured some of the more quixotic behaviors of the famous desperado. In 1942, Copland followed it with *Rodeo*, a ballet choreographed by Agnes de Mille, depicting dance movements by members in cowboy garb. Several numbers emanating from the production included the famous "Hoe-Down," a tune so explicitly Western that it is difficult for audiences to conjure anything but cowboys, chaps, boots, and bucking broncos.

Like Copland, Puccini, Berlin, and Rodgers and Hammerstein, Craig Bohmler thought he could produce the quintessential Western work of art by adapting *Riders of the Purple Sage* for the stage. "It spoke so strongly to me," Bohmler told the *Arizona Republic*. "The heightened emotions, the woman alone, combating the society in which she finds herself. Enter the gunfighter to avenge the death of his sister, who had her child taken away from her and then died of a broken heart."[1] With its operatic flourishes and stunning landscapes, *Riders* seemed to fit the bill perfectly. Bohmler was not a newcomer to the field; indeed, he had written several first-rate operas, but in this case he shaped *Riders* for a debut by the Arizona Opera, which intended on giving the production its world premiere.

In the Western tradition of Elmer Bernstein's theme music for *The Magnificent Seven* and other musical classics, Bohmler began writing a lushly romantic score and enlisted Steven Mark Kohn to create the libretto. Gradually, the opera took form, sweeping investors, producers, and technicians into its forward momentum. The goal was to launch Bohmler's opera in late February 2017, first in Tucson and then in Phoenix. Famed Arizona artist Ed Mell was approached to design and create the dynamic Western backdrops. At *Riders of the Purple Sage*'s world premiere, crowds surged in. The combination of Bohmler's music and Kohn's writing, the vivid period costumes, the flashy choreography, and Mell's dreamy, flamboyant landscapes helped make it an Arizona—and a world—success.

But the true test of an opera is whether it can be repeated and then enter the repertory. Less than 10 percent of these artistic works can boast of even making it to a fourth production. But the signs are strong for *Riders* to endure on the stage. In 2017, it brought in more money than Bizet's

Carmen, staged the previous year, and became one of the highest-grossing productions in the history of the Arizona Opera. All indications are that *Riders of the Purple Sage* will return to Phoenix and treat audiences well into the third decade of the century.

This sixth adaptation of Grey's classic demonstrates that its strong romantic elements can be reworked for film and stage. Who knows what other forms it will take in the future? What is certain is that it has great legs—human, equine, and theatrical.

* * *

Before there was *Riders of the Purple Sage*, or *The Heritage of the Desert*, or even *Betty Zane*, there was Pearl Zane Grey living on Grubstreet in upper Manhattan. He was a dentist then, probably the best tooth puller in the area, or so he thought. He had a strong right arm—his baseball pitching arm—that he used to extract reluctant molars. As a youth, he had kept that arm in shape by tossing fifty baseballs a day into an apple basket. In 1900, after four years in New York City, he was established and handsome enough to meet suitable young women. He admitted, half-heartedly, that he was a dentist, which no doubt appealed to women seeking a good provider.

Dentistry brought in the money, but for Grey it was not what dreams are made of. In his heart, at least, he moved into Grubstreet and began his long apprenticeship in the written word. He met Dolly, who seemed far more capable and intellectual than any other woman he had ever met. She was also willing to help steer him through some of the more adverse years for a writer.

In 1906 he saw the West for the first time, and the scenery was compelling enough to bring him back—again and again. His years of preparation, and the many rejections he had received along the way, laid the groundwork for his first major success in 1910, the year *The Heritage of the Desert* appeared. Often his fictional characters stemmed from real people and sometimes they sprung from his imagination. But all of them were people of the frontier: cowboys, Navajo guides, traders, cattlemen, sheep men, newcomers, veterans, and wanderers of the wasteland. Rising above all of them was the terrain, sometimes bleak and hostile, other times majestic and forbidding, but always a character in the human drama.

Other writers of the era chose to depict the West in different terms, their work falling somewhere along the romanticist/realist spectrum. Grey served up a potent, fast-paced brand of romanticism that people liked, and judging by the success of the sixth adaptation of *Riders of the Purple Sage*, it would seem they still do. He said his novels were as authentic as any other writer's. He was right. Few authors could claim that they had traveled more in the West than Zane Grey, and few had experienced the life that he found deep in the high desert.

Fictional characters usually exercise their right to be more real than those we know intimately. Authors realize this, so they try to make their heroes and heroines as dynamic as possible. Jim Lassiter and Jane Withersteen are cases in point. They linger in our memory and visit us at the most inopportune times. What does Lassiter, the man in black riding a near-blind horse, a man from somewhere with obscure motives, really seek? To avenge his sister's death? To love a woman? To sleep peacefully out on the sage?

We don't know. But regardless of motive, we discover in the novel that we are satisfied with his quest.

And then there is Jane Withersteen: proud, beautiful, whimsical, and somewhat vain. As the central figure in the novel, she radiates energy, attracting a whole world of evil and goodness. Her currents run deep. In the midst of chaos, she has the faith and courage to find her path. She learns to trust the very core of herself that lies somewhere between the heart and the head.

They live out in the remote spaces of Zane Grey's West, a place where time does not tick.

The present, past, and future slip into each other. The heavens shake the stars loose and the old sun returns like a hot iron to sear the wounds of another day. But those who know this land often pause and listen to the voices that rise beyond the sage and stone pillars.

"'Lassiter! Roll the stone!' she cried. He arose, tottering, but with set face, and again he placed the bloody hand on the Balancing Rock. . . . '*Roll the Stone! . . . Lassiter, I love you!*'"

Yes, Mr. Grey, we are in the Old West now.

ENDNOTES

Chapter One: Grubstreet, USA
1. Ronald Weber, *Hired Pens*, 17.
2. Ibid., 21.
3. Ibid., 65.
4. Ibid., 66.
5. Ibid., 87.
6. Ibid., 67.
7. Zane Grey's diary, 30 April 1917.
8. Zane Grey, *Tales of Lonely Trails*, 181.
9. Zane Grey's diary, 1 June 1926.
10. Zane Grey's diary, 24 January 1920.
11. Frank Gruber, *Zane Grey: A Biography*, 23.
12. Frank Munsey, letter to Zane Grey, 16 May 1903.
13. Weber, 99.
14. Ibid., 127.
15. Ibid., 301.
16. Ibid., 310.
17. Ibid., 218.
18. Ibid., 176.

Chapter Two: Beloved Infidel
1. George Reiger, *Zane Grey: Outdoorsman*, 2–4.
2. Zane Grey, letter to Dolly Roth, 2 September 1902.
3. Dolly Roth, letter to Zane Grey, 20 October 1901.
4. Ibid.
5. Zane Grey's diary, 30 April 1917.
6. Zane Grey, letter to Dolly Roth, 19 October 1903.
7. Zane Grey, letter to Dolly Roth, 27 September 1904.
8. Dolly Grey, letter to Zane Grey, 3 January 1904.
9. Zane Grey, letter to Dolly Grey, 1 October 1905.
10. Zane Grey, letter to Dolly Grey, 28 October 1905.
11. Zane Grey's diary, 11 January 1906.

Chapter Three: Way Out There
1. Zane Grey, letter to Dolly Grey, 26 March 1908.
2. Zane Grey, letter to Dolly Grey, 2 April 1907.

3. Zane Grey, letter to Dolly Grey, 12 April 1907.
4. Zane Grey, letter to Dolly Grey, 27 March 1907.
5. Zane Grey, letter to Dolly Grey, 12 April 1907.
6. Zane Grey, "The Man Who Influenced Me Most," *American Magazine*, August 1926: 136.
7. Ibid.
8. Zane Grey, letter to E. D. Woolley, 18 October 1908.
9. Zane Grey, *The Last of the Plainsmen*, 19.
10. Ibid., 21.
11. Ibid., 22.
12. Ibid., 21.
13. Ibid., 25.
14. Ibid., 27.
15. Ibid., 28.
16. Zane Grey, "The Man Who Influenced Me Most," 136.
17. Zane Grey, *The Last of the Plainsmen*, 30.
18. Ibid., 31.
19. Ibid., 32.
20. Ibid., 40–41.
21. Ibid., 137.
22. Ibid., 138.
23. Ibid., 123–124.

Chapter Four: The Reckoning

1. Zane Grey's diary, 14 February 1908.
2. Ibid.
3. Quoted in Carlton Jackson, *Zane Grey*, 1.
4. Zane Grey's diary, 2 February 1908.
5. Will Bagley, *Blood of the Prophets*, 20.
6. Ibid., 141.
7. Ibid., 143.
8. Ibid., 153.
9. Quoted in Bagley, 153.
10. Ibid., 155.
11. Ibid., 176.
12. Ibid., 262.
13. Ibid., 263.
14. Ibid., 264.
15. Ibid., 265.

Chapter Five: The House of Harper

1. Ronald Weber, *Hired Pens*, 87.
2. Clayton Hamilton, *Materials and Methods of Fiction*, 46.

3. Mark Twain, "Fenimore Cooper's Literary Offenses," *New England Quarterly*, September 1946, 291–98.
4. Ibid., 296.
5. Hamilton, 43.
6. Zane Grey, "The Man Who Influenced Me Most," 53.
7. Herman Melville, *White Jacket*, 54.
8. D. H. Lawrence, *Studies in Classic American Literature*, 131.
9. Eugene Exman, *The House of Harper*, 153.
10. Owen Wister, *The Virginian*, 10.
11. Owen Wister, "Hank's Woman," *Harper's Weekly*, October 1892, 34.

Chapter Six: A Horseman Riding By

1. Quoted in Gruber, 99.
2. Ibid., 101.
3. Zane Grey's diary, 2 March 1910.
4. Hamilton, 72.
5. Ibid., 56.
6. *Life*, August 1911, 31.
7. Zane Grey, *The Heritage of the Desert*, 58.
8. Zane Grey's diary, 10 April 1910.
9. Zane Grey, *Tales of Lonely Trails*, 6.

Chapter Seven: Inside Riders

1. Hamilton, 67.
2. Zane Grey, *Riders of the Purple Sage*, 9.
3. Hamilton, 23.
4. Zane Grey, *Riders of the Purple Sage*, 14.
5. Ibid., 57.
6. Ibid., 15.
7. Ibid., 9.
8. Ibid., 8.
9. Ibid., 190.
10. Ibid., 113
11. Ibid., 107.
12. Ibid., 113.
13. Ibid., 152.
14. Ibid., 154.
15. Ibid., 216.
16. Ibid., 218.
17. Ibid., 219.
18. Ibid., 245.
19. Ibid.
20. Ibid., 280.

Chapter Eight: After the Rainbow
1. Dolly Grey's diary, 31 December 1913.
2. Lillian Wilhelm's diary, 3 April 1913.
3. Zane Grey, *Tales of Lonely Trails*, 4.
4. Ibid., 5.
5. Ibid., 6.
6. Ibid., 7.
7. Ibid.
8. Ibid., 9.
9. Ibid.
10. Ibid., 15.
11 Zane Grey, *The Light of Western Stars*, 4.
12. Ibid.
13. Dolly Grey, letter to Zane Grey, 11 March 1913.
14. Zane Grey, *The Rainbow Trail*, 250.
15. Ibid., 14.
16. Ibid., 61.
17. Ibid., 200.
18. Ibid., 67.
19. Ibid.
20. Ibid., 59.
21. Ibid., 61.
22. Ibid., 123.
23. Ibid., 212.
24. Ibid., 232.
25. Ibid., 235.
26. Ibid., 233.
27. Zane Grey, *Riders of the Purple Sage*, 97–98.
28. Zane Grey's diary, 15 July 1910.
29. Hamilton, 103.

Chapter Nine: Silent Riders
1. Bob Davis, letter to Zane Grey, 7 February 1916.
2. Weber, 97.
3. Ibid., 98.
4. *Motion Picture News*, 6 September 1916.
5. *Variety*, 18 October 1918.
6. *Motion Picture News*, 8 November 1918.
7. Zane Grey's diary, 14 April 1917.
8. Ibid., 30 April 1917.
9. Zane Grey, letter to Dolly Grey, 21 September 1916.
10. Dolly Grey, letter to Zane Grey, 21 August 1916.
11. Zane Grey, letter to Dolly Grey, 28 August 1916.
12. Zane Grey's diary, 9 January 1919.

13. Ibid., 29 May 1919.
14. Ibid., 23 November 1920.
15. Ibid., 21 January 1921.
16. *New York Times*, 20 March 1925.
17. *Variety*, 25 June 1925.
18. Zane Grey's diary, 2 May 1925.

Chapter Ten: Riders *Redux*

1. Quoted in Ed Hulse, *Filming the West of Zane Grey*, 186–87.
2. Zane Grey, letter to Dolly Grey, 21 February 1939.
3. *The New York Times*, 10 May 1943.
4. Ibid., 18 April 2002.
5. Ibid., 25 July 1952.
6. Ibid., 24 April 1953.
7. Roger Ebert, *Chicago Sun-Times*, 3 September 2000.
8. *TV Guide*, 5 January 1996

Epilogue: Riders, Ride On!

1. *Arizona Republic*, 20 February 2017.

Selected Sources

Collections

Anschutz Collection, Denver, Colorado
Cline Library, Northern Arizona University
HarperCollins archives
New York Public Library
Oho Historical Society, Columbus, Ohio
Zane Grey's West Society

Books

Bagley, Will. *Blood of the Prophets*. Norman: University of Oklahoma Press, 2005.
Exman, Eugene. *The House of Harper*. New York: Harper & Row, 1967.
Grey, Zane. *Betty Zane*. New York: Charles Francis Press, 1903.
———. *The Last of the Plainsmen*. New York: Outing Publishing Co., 1908.
———. *The Heritage of the Desert*. New York: Harper and Brothers, 1910.
———. *Riders of the Purple Sage*. New York: Harper and Brothers, 1912.
———. *The Light Western Stars*. New York: Harper and Brothers, 1914.
———. "The Desert Crucible." *Argosy*, 1915.
———. *The Rainbow Trail*. New York: Harper and Brothers, 1915.
———. *Tales of Lonely Trails*. New York: Harper and Brothers, 1922.
Gruber, Frank. *Zane Grey: A Biography*. New York: Tower Books, 1969.
Hamilton, Clayton. *Materials and Methods of Fiction*. New York: Baker & Taylor, 1908.
Hulse, Ed. *Filming the West of Zane Grey*. Nashville, TN: Riverwood Press, 2016.
Jackson, Carlton. *Zane Grey*. United States Authors, vol. 218. Woodbridge, CT: Twayne, 1983.
Kant, Candace, ed. *The Letters of Zane and Dolly Grey*. Reno: University of Nevada Press, 2008.
Lawrence, D. H. *Studies in Classic American Literature*. [NY]: Viking, 1922.
Lyon, Thomas, ed. *Literary History of the American West*. Fort Worth: Texas Christian University Press, 2003.
May, Stephen J. *Zane Grey: Romancing the West*. Athens: Ohio University Press, 1997.
———. *Maverick Heart: The Further Adventures of Zane Grey*. Athens: Ohio University Press, 2000.
Melville, Herman. *White Jacket*. New York: Harper and Brothers, 1850.
Pauly, Thomas. *Zane Grey, His Life, His Work*. Chicago: University of Illinois Press, 2005.
Reiger, George, ed. *Zane Grey: Outdoorsman*. Mechanicsburg, PA: Stackpole Books, 2007.

Speer, Albert. *Inside the Third Reich*. New York: Simon & Schuster, 1997.
Tuska, Jon. *The Filming of the West*. New York: Doubleday & Co., 1976.
Twain, Mark. *The Mysterious Stranger*. New York: Harper and Brothers, 1922.
Weber, Ronald. *Hired Pens*. Athens: Ohio University Press, 1997.

MANUSCRIPTS

"Riders of the Purple Sage," 1911, Ohio Historical Society
"The Desert Crucible," 1914, Ohio Historical Society

Index

Italicized page numbers indicate photographs.

ABOUT THE AUTHOR

STEPHEN J. MAY IS A LITERARY CRITIC, BIOGRAPHER, FEATURE WRITER, novelist, and art enthusiast. His writing subjects include the Western adventures and novels of Zane Grey (*Romancing the West, Maverick Heart*); the war experiences of Pulitzer Prize–winning author James A. Michener (*Michener: A Writer's Journey*) and how they shaped the legendary Broadway hit *South Pacific* (*Michener's South Pacific*); the history of Colorado's first family, the Palmers of Glen Eyrie (*A Kingdom of Their Own*); and the slave trade's influence on one of the great paintings of the nineteenth century, J. M. W. Turner's *The Slave Ship* (*Voyage of The Slave Ship*). He lives in Sedona, Arizona.